Mother of Sweet Bliss

By Swami Amritaswarupananda

Mata Amritanandamayi Center, San Ramon
California, United States

Mother of Sweet Bliss

Published by
  Mata Amritanandamayi Center
  P.O. Box 613
  San Ramon, CA 94583
  United States

First edition by the MA Centre: 2015

In India:
  www.amritapuri.org
  inform@amritapuri.org

In US:
  www.amma.org

In Europe:
  www.amma-europe.org

Contents

Part one

Biography

Chapter one

The Divine Child

In India, on the southern coast of Kerala, there is a tiny village called Parayakadavu. It lies on a narrow strip of land covered with coconut trees between the Arabian Sea on one side, and the backwaters on the other. The people of this village have been fishermen for as long as anyone can remember. There are many stories of the holiness and greatness of Parayakadavu going back to ancient times.

In this place, many years ago, a thirteen-year-old boy called Sugunanandan Idammanel had just come home from school and was climbing a cashew tree with his cousin. They were busy eating the delicious cashew fruits when they suddenly saw a monk with long hair and a long flowing beard walking beneath the tree. He was wearing the traditional orange robes of a Hindu monk. They had never seen him before, and they were filled with wonder, for his face glowed with a beautiful light. The monk suddenly burst into joyful laughter, saying loudly to himself, "Many monks will attain *samadhi* (a state of oneness with God) here. They will see God. This will become a holy place!" The monk laughed blissfully and continued on his way. They never saw him again.

Sugunanandan and his cousin were puzzled. What could the monk have meant when he said that this place, the home of Sugunanandan's family, would one day become a holy place? Only many years later did Sugunanandan understand the meaning of those words.

Sugunanandan's family belonged to a clan of fishermen. They had been fishermen for generations and were very religious.

When Sugunanandan grew up he became a fishmonger, selling the fish that the fishermen caught in the sea. He married Damayanti, a young woman from a nearby village. Damayanti also came from a very religious family.

Damayanti and Sugunanandan had eight children – four boys and four girls. When Damayanti was expecting her third child, she began having strange, wonderful dreams. In those dreams, Lord Krishna, Lord Shiva and the Divine Mother appeared to her. One night she dreamed that a mysterious being gave her a beautiful statue of Krishna made of pure gold. Sugunanandan also had a dream in which he saw the Divine Mother. Sugunanandan and Damayanti talked to each other about their dreams and wondered what they could mean. They thought that perhaps something very special was about to happen in their lives. Little did they know what God had planned for them.

One night Damayanti had the most wonderful dream. She dreamed that she gave birth to a child more beautiful than any child on earth, and the child was Krishna. She held the Divine Baby in her arms. Damayanti wasn't expecting her child to be born for some time yet. When the time came she planned to go to her parents' house and give birth there. But the next day, when she was working down at the seashore, she suddenly had a strong feeling that she should go home. She stopped working and went home by herself. She then realized that she was about to give birth.

At that time, Damayanti and her husband were living in a simple hut. As soon as Damayanti entered the hut, she lay down on a straw mat and the child was born. It happened very quickly and Damayanti felt no pain. She noticed that the child didn't cry the way babies usually do when they are born. Damayanti looked at the child and saw that it was a baby girl. She was filled with wonder when she saw the beaming smile on the baby's face. She would never forget the way the baby looked at her. It was a look that seemed to know everything, a look so powerful and so loving, it reached right into her heart.

A neighbour woman who happened to pass by looked in through the door. As soon as she realized what had happened, she came inside and took care of Damayanti and the newborn baby.

Thus it was that on the morning of 27th September, 1953, the Holy Mother was born in a simple hut made of plaited palm leaves. Not far from the hut the ocean waves danced joyfully against the shore, and in the nearby backwaters, the tiny waves lapped softly against the bank. It sounded as if Mother Nature was singing a welcoming lullaby to the newborn child.

The little girl showed many signs of being a divine child – signs that no one understood at the time. She lay with her legs crossed in a lotus posture, and her little fingers formed a *mudra*, which is a holy sign. The child was darker than the other members of the family, and her skin had a dark-blue shade. Her parents were puzzled by this. They thought there must be something wrong with her. They went to several doctors, but the doctors couldn't understand why the baby's skin was so blue. They thought she must be suffering from some strange, unknown disease. They told Damayanti not to give the child a bath for six months, thinking that this would somehow make the baby's colour normal. Damayanti did exactly as the doctors told her, but it didn't help. The blue tone stayed on the baby's skin for a long time.

The parents gave their baby daughter the name Sudhamani, which means "Pure Jewel." She was a very unusual child. Unlike other babies, she started speaking when she was only six months old. She also started walking at that time. Before a baby learns to walk, it will first crawl for a few months, and then when the child is about a year old, it will finally have learned how to stand up and walk. But Sudhamani was different. She never went through a crawling stage at all. One day, when she was six months old, she was sitting on the veranda of the new house that the family had just built. She suddenly stood up and walked straight across the veranda! Soon thereafter she amazed everyone when she began to run.

Right from the start, Sudhamani loved Lord Krishna more than anything in the world. As soon as she learned to speak, she started saying the name, "Krishna, Krishna," over and over again. When she was just two years old, she started praying to the Lord, and she loved to sing little songs to him – songs that she made up herself. She sang to Krishna every day. By the age of four, she was singing her little songs with intense love and devotion, sitting before a small picture of Krishna. This picture was her greatest treasure. She always kept it tucked inside her blouse, and she would take it out and look at it, again and again.

Her love for the Lord continued to grow. By the time she was five, her heart was overflowing with devotion. Her beautiful way of singing became known throughout the neighbourhood. Whenever she sang her songs, she gazed at her little picture of Krishna. She never got tired of looking at it.

Sudhamani was often thinking so much about the Lord that she completely forgot about everything around her. Her parents would find her sitting all alone somewhere – sitting absolutely still with her eyes closed. Sometimes they found her sitting beside the backwaters, staring at the water, or quietly gazing up at the blue sky. She seemed to be in another world.

But instead of treasuring this very special little girl, the whole family turned against her because she was so different, and also because her skin was darker than theirs.

Her parents didn't understand her intense devotion towards the Lord – they thought it wasn't normal. They couldn't understand why their little daughter was singing to Krishna all the time, often dancing round and round in a circle as she sang, unaware of the world around her. And whenever she went into a state of bliss, which she often did, they thought she was playing a silly game. They scolded her for not being like other children. They often treated her very badly, scolding her and hitting her for the smallest thing. Whenever her parents went out to visit relatives or to take part in a religious festival, they usually took all their children along with them, except Sudhamani. She was told to stay at home and take care of the house and the animals. To them she was no more than a servant. It was as if she didn't really belong to her own family. But Sudhamani had no complaints. She liked to be alone and it was a good opportunity for her to think about Sri Krishna.

There was a cowshed next to the house. Sudhamani loved to sit there all by herself, with just the cows for company. In there she sang her songs to Krishna, and meditated and prayed to him with all her heart and soul. Sudhamani was happy in the cowshed. She loved the cows just as the Divine Cowherd Boy, Krishna, had once loved them.

Sudhamani started school at the age of five. Though she was so young, her teachers soon noticed how unusually intelligent she was. She needed only to hear a lesson once to remember everything that had been said. She could also easily repeat anything that she had read. When she was in the second grade, she sometimes listened to a lesson being given to the older children in the higher classes, and afterwards she could easily recite those lessons as well. The older children, including her older brother and sister, were sometimes punished by the teacher because they couldn't learn a poem by heart. Sudhamani, on the other hand, who was much younger, would happily sing that same poem while she danced to the tune like a delicate butterfly. The teachers were very fond of her. They were amazed at her unusual memory power; they had never seen anything like it. She received the highest marks in every subject. She was the best student in her class, even though she was often forced to stay at home to help her mother with the household work.

Sudhamani was full of life and energy. The villagers affectionately called her "Kunju" [the little one]. They loved her because of her noble character – her intense devotion towards the Lord, the way she loved all of God's creatures, her kindness towards the poor and the suffering, and her sweet, melodious singing. She was also very good at listening to people. Those who met her found that their hearts opened up when they talked to her, and they would tell her all about their problems, even though she was so young. Even strangers felt drawn to her the moment they saw her.

Sudhamani got up every morning long before the sun rose and greeted the Lord with her song. All the neighbours found the little girl's voice so pure and sweet and enchanting that they tried to wake up early every morning, so that they could hear her greet the Lord and the new day.

Many of Sudhamani's most beautiful songs were sad songs, because she sang about her longing for Krishna. It was extremely painful for her to be separated from the Lord. In her songs she called out to him, she pleaded with him to come to her, telling him how much she longed to see him. Whenever she sang those songs, tears trickled down her cheeks. She wept and wept until she felt her heart would break. The neighbours were worried when they saw this, and some of them tried to console her. But only Krishna could console the little one. Only Krishna could make her happy. The villagers understood that Sudhamani was in a different world.

But her family had little sympathy for her and often treated her badly.

Although her father often mistreated her – mainly because he didn't understand her –deep in his heart he loved his daughter very much. Sometimes Sudhamani felt an intense longing to leave everything – to leave her home, her family and everything she knew – and just meditate on Krishna all the time. She thought about the sacred Himalayan mountains, where the yogis sat in caves and meditated all day long. One night she said to her father, "Father, take me to a lonely place! Take me to the Himalayas!" and she started crying. It was a very long way to the Himalayas, which are in the very northern part of India, so, of course, he couldn't take her there. But just to stop her crying, he held her against his shoulder and said, "I will take you there soon. Get some sleep now, my child!" Sudhamani felt comforted and fell asleep with her head on his shoulder, believing that he would take her there right away. But when she woke up a little later, she began to cry again, because she saw that he hadn't taken her to the Himalayas, and that they were still in their little fishing village surrounded by coconut trees.

When Sudhamani couldn't sleep at night and insisted on meditating out in the courtyard, her father would stay up and watch over her to make sure that she was safe.

Chapter two

The Little Saint

Sudhamani went to school only for four years. When she was ten years old, her mother became ill with rheumatism, which meant that Sudhamani had to stay at home and do all the household work. She had always helped her mother a great deal, but now she suddenly had to do all the work by herself.

Sudhamani had to get up at three o'clock every morning. Sometimes, when she was very tired, she accidentally overslept. When this happened, her mother got angry and woke her up by pouring a jug of cold water over her head.

Sudhamani worked hard all day long and late into the evening. She cleaned the house and swept the yard outside. She had to go all the way to the village well to fetch drinking water. She cooked food for the family, scrubbed the pots and pans, washed everyone's clothes, looked after the cows and milked them, and cared for the goats and ducks. Even for a grown-up person this would have been very hard work – and Sudhamani was just a child. But she never complained, not even a little. Though she was busy working all day long, her mind was always on Krishna. She never forgot him even for a moment. Her lips were always

moving as she said the name, "Krishna, Krishna," again and again. If she ever heard anyone just mention the name, "Krishna," she felt so much love in her heart that her eyes would fill with tears.

No matter what sort of work Sudhamani was doing, she always imagined she was doing it for the Lord. She did everything for him. When she washed the family's clothes, she imagined that she was washing Krishna's clothes. When she hung the clothes out on the line to dry, she pretended that they were Krishna's yellow silk clothes glittering in the sun. When she dressed her little brothers and sisters for school, she imagined that they were Krishna and his brother, Balarama. When she took care of the cows, she thought about the Divine Cowherd Boy, Gopala Krishna, who looked after the cows in the fields and forests of Vrindavan.

She still carried her little picture of the Lord wherever she went, and often looked at it. She would hug the picture close to her and kiss it, and then she would cry because she longed so much to see the real Krishna and to be with him. She cried until the picture was wet with her tears. She knew that there was nothing more beautiful than Krishna, and that he was more loving than all the people in the world put together. She longed with all her heart to see him, to play with him and dance with him. She wanted to be with him forever.

Sudhamani spent a lot of time carrying water, washing clothes and wading through the backwaters to pick grass for the cows. Because of this, her clothes were usually wet. She often had to carry heavy pots of water and hot rice gruel for the cows – which she carried on her head, the Indian way – and because of this, her hair fell out on the top of her head.

Even though Sudhamani worked very hard and always tried to do her best, her mother often scolded her and gave her a beating for the smallest mistake. Years later, when Sudhamani was grown up and looked back on her childhood, she said, "Damayanti was, in a way, my guru[1]. She taught me self-discipline and how to do everything with great care. If a single straw fell out of the broom when I was sweeping, or if there happened to be a tiny bit of rubbish still lying on the ground after I had finished sweeping the courtyard, I was punished. I was also punished if a speck of dust or ash happened to fall into the pot while I was cooking over the fire, or if the slightest trace of dirt was found in a pot after I had washed the dishes. Sometimes Damayanti even hit me with a wooden pestle. When other people saw how badly I was being treated, they said to Damayanti, 'Please don't punish her like that.' But Damayanti wouldn't listen to them."

Sometimes Damayanti tried to frighten Sudhamani. She said, "Here comes a ghost! It's coming to get you!" But no one could frighten the little one, because she wasn't scared of anything. She was very courageous.

There was an old woman in the village called Apisil who liked to frighten small children. If the children were naughty, their parents would call Apisil to come and frighten them so that they would behave themselves. One day Damayanti asked Apisil to come and scare Sudhamani. The old woman covered her head with a sack and sneaked up to the window where Sudhamani happened to be sitting. Then the horrible-looking Apisil jumped up and down and howled and shrieked and did everything she could to frighten the little one. But Sudhamani wasn't scared at all. She looked bravely out through the window at the jumping, screaming monster and said, "Go away! I know who you are. You're just Apisil. Don't try to frighten me!" Damayanti called Apisil a few times, but the little one was never frightened.

Sudhamani's older brother, Subhagan, was such a bad-tempered boy that the whole family, and even the villagers, were afraid of him. He was proud of the fact that he didn't believe

---

[1] A guru is a spiritual teacher.

in God. He also thought that boys were better than girls, and that girls should be seen and not heard. He was especially cruel to Sudhamani and was always looking for an excuse to punish her for something. He couldn't stand her devotion to Krishna or the way she sang to the Lord. Just to hear her made him angry.

Because Sudhamani was busy working all day long and late into the evening, it was only at night that she had time to sit by herself and worship the Lord. By then it was so late that the oil lamp in the *puja* room[2] had burnt out. So Sudhamani sat in the dark and sang her songs. When Subhagan noticed what she was doing, he got angry at her for sitting like that in the dark, and he shouted at her. Sudhamani said to him, "You can see only the outer light. But deep inside me there is a light that can never go out!" Subhagan didn't understand that she was talking about the Divine Light, a light more bright and beautiful than any ordinary light, and that this light was always shining deep within her.

As part of her household duties, Sudhamani often visited the neighbouring houses to collect vegetable scraps and rice gruel for the cows. Sudhamani listened patiently to the many sad tales of the elderly people who lived there. They often told her how their grown-up children and grandchildren, who once had prayed for their health and long life, were now neglecting and ill-treating them. The old people were very lonely and had no one to talk to. Sudhamani listened to them with great attention. She felt so sorry for them. She always tried to spend some time with the old ones because no one loved them or cared about them. When she heard their stories, she came to understand how selfish human beings are, and that there is hardly any real love or compassion to be found in the world.

---

[2] In Indian homes, there is often a special room for worship, called a puja room.

But Sudhamani's own heart was filled with compassion. Her heart went out to those who were sad and poor and lonely. Though only a child, she did whatever she could to ease the suffering of her elderly neighbours. Sometimes, when no one was at home, she would go and fetch one of the neglected old women and take her home with her. She lovingly gave the old one a hot bath, dressed her in clothes belonging to Sudhamani's family, and fed her with whatever food she could find.

Whenever Sudhamani came to know of anyone in the village who didn't have enough food, she tried to help them. She took some money from her mother's money box and bought them some food. If this wasn't possible, she stubbornly pestered her father until he gave her a little money. If this also failed, she took some raw vegetables and rice from the storeroom and gave it to the family in need. One day she was caught red-handed as she took some food for a starving man. Though she was beaten severely, she secretly continued giving food to the poor, because she couldn't bear to see anyone suffer.

Whenever she stole some milk, she would add water to the remaining milk, to make up for the loss so that no one would notice that any was missing. Damayanti didn't know that the food and milk that Sudhamani took were being given to the destitute families that she befriended.

Sometimes, when Sudhamani was out walking, she came across children who were undernourished and wandering about by themselves because their parents were unable to look after them properly. Sudhamani would take them home with her. She fed them and cleaned them, and then she took them back to their homes.

Sudhamani's brothers and sisters took advantage of her goodheartedness. They often stole snacks from the kitchen, and whenever Damayanti noticed that something was missing, they pointed at Sudhamani and said, "She did it!" Though Sudhamani knew who the real thieves were, she didn't say a word to defend herself. She just kept quiet and allowed Damayanti to punish her for what the others had done. Sometimes her brothers and sisters felt bad about what they had done and confessed to their parents that the little one was innocent. Sudhamani's parents would then ask her why she had taken the blame and punishment without saying a word in her own defence. Sudhamani would say, "I don't mind suffering for others, for the mistakes they've made in their ignorance."

One day Sudhamani came across a very poor family. They didn't have anything to eat. Sudhamani desperately wanted to help them. She tried to find them some food, but there was nothing in the house, and she couldn't find any money either. She felt that she couldn't just leave the family to starve, so she took a gold bracelet belonging to her mother and gave it to them. When her father came home and found out what she had done, he exploded with anger. He tied the little one to a tree and whipped her until her thin little body was bleeding.

Even though Sudhamani was treated like this, she never resented anyone. She loved God so much that she couldn't help loving everyone else as well. She even loved those who treated her badly. She felt that everyone was a part of God. She believed that whatever happened to her was God's will, even if it was painful – and so she accepted it. Instead of making her feel angry, her suffering made her turn more and more towards her beloved Krishna; it made her long for him more than anything in the world. She came to understand that only God was her real friend, and that only God was her real Mother and Father.

Because Sudhamani felt the same love for everyone, she called all women, "mother," and all men, "father." Her father, Sugunanandan, didn't like this. He scolded her for calling other people father and mother. The little one said to him, "I have never seen my real Mother and Father, so I feel that everyone is my mother and father."

Though the villagers were very fond of Sudhamani, she wasn't especially close to anyone. She felt that Krishna was her best friend. She also had a very special love for animals. When she looked at the cows, goats, dogs, birds and all the other creatures, she could see her beloved Krishna shining in all of them. She talked to the animals, imagining that they were Krishna. In this way she told the Lord all her problems. Sometimes when a cow was lying down resting, Sudhamani would lie down next to it. She would curl up close to the cow and lay her head on its body, imagining that she was lying on Krishna's lap.

Chapter three

Working as a Servant

A s the years went by, Sudhamani continued to work for her family. But all the time, night and day, her mind was on her beloved Krishna. Sudhamani was now thirteen years old.

It was difficult for people to find servants in the area. When Sudhamani's relatives needed a servant, it was decided that Sudhamani should go and work for her grandmother and her aunts and uncles.

Her grandmother's house was six kilometres away. To get there, one could either travel by boat or walk along the beach. Every day Sudhamani travelled to and from her grandmother's house in a little ferry boat. As she sat in the boat, she greatly enjoyed looking down at the blue water, imagining that she could see Krishna smiling at her in the water. Sudhamani liked to chant the sacred sound "Om" together with the humming sound of the boat engine. When she did this, her heart overflowed with so much joy that she soon burst into song. The other passengers in the boat greatly enjoyed her singing.

One day Damayanti stopped giving her money for the boat ride. "You can just as well walk," she said to Sudhamani. The little one wasn't sad about this at all. She said to herself, "There's no reason for me to be unhappy. Now that I have to walk all the way, I have a chance to be alone during that time and then I can think about God."

So the next morning she started walking along the seashore towards her grandmother's house. Whenever Sudhamani listened to the ocean, it sounded as if the waves were chanting the holy sound, "Om." So, on this morning, as she walked along the beach, she heard the waves slowly singing, "Om... Om... Om...," and it made her feel so close to God that she was overwhelmed with bliss. As she walked, she began to sing a song to the Lord. As she looked out at the ocean, the blue water reminded her of the blue-coloured Krishna. She looked up at the sky where soft, blue-grey clouds floated by. Their colour also reminded her of him. As she gazed at the sea and the sky, she began to long so much for the Lord that she burst into tears. Her mind was so full of Krishna that she completely forgot about the world around her. Again she looked out across the water, but all she could see was Krishna! And oh how beautiful he was! Krishna was in every wave of the ocean. Sudhamani stumbled to the edge of the water and tried to hug the waves, thinking that she was hugging Krishna. With her clothes dripping wet, she then continued walking along the beach, loudly calling his name. "Krishna! Oh Krishna!" she called, again and again. She was filled with so much love for him that she no longer knew what she was doing. Her steps became slower and slower until she finally stopped and fell onto the sand. There she lay, not knowing where she was. She couldn't see the sand or the sea or the sky – there was only Krishna. The Lord was everywhere, and she was bathing in bliss. She had forgotten that she was supposed to go to her grandmother's house. Some hours later, when she finally remembered where she was, she got up and continued on her way. It happened many times that she was delayed in this way.

At her grandmother's house, Sudhamani was given a lot of work to do. She did her best and worked as hard as she could. Her grandmother was very pleased with her and treated her kindly. One day the little one was sent to a grain mill to husk rice paddy. On the way there, she had to pass through a village where many families were so poor that they didn't have enough to eat. Sudhamani felt heartbroken when she saw how they were suffering. Later, as she walked home from the mill, she met a family who hadn't eaten anything for three days. Without a moment's hesitation, she gave them some of the rice she was carrying. When she returned to the house, her grandmother noticed that some of the rice was missing. She asked the little one to explain. But Sudhamani didn't want her grandmother to know that she had helped anyone. She was afraid that if she did, her grandmother might go and quarrel with the poor family, and then they would feel humiliated. So in order to protect them, she didn't say a word. Her grandmother thought the little one must have sold the rice and bought herself some sweets with the money. So Sudhamani was punished. It happened a few more times that her grandmother noticed that some rice was missing. But no matter how much the little one was punished, she never revealed what she had done.

It made Sudhamani happy that her grandmother also loved Krishna. A big picture of the Lord hung in one of the rooms of the house. Whenever Sudhamani had a free moment, she went and stood in front of it. Sudhamani's uncle loved her very much, and when he saw her standing there singing to the picture, he brought her a stool to sit on. But the little one didn't want to sit. She pointed at the picture and said, "Look, uncle! Krishna is standing. How can I sit when he is standing?" To Sudhamani, the picture was not made of paper and paint – it was the real Krishna standing in front of her in flesh and blood.

Her grandmother's neighbours were charmed by Sudhamani's songs. They often came over to the house just to listen to her sing. Their hearts were filled with devotion when they heard her compositions. They gradually learned the songs and began singing them in their own *puja* rooms.

The seasons came and went. The following year Sudhamani was sent to work for her aunt. As usual, she was given a huge amount of work to do. Her cousins considered it shameful to do any household work. The older ones didn't believe in God and whenever they got a chance they teased the little one mercilessly because of her love for Krishna. They also tried to stop her from singing her songs. When they managed to prevent Sudhamani from singing, she would hide her face in her hands and burst into tears. They could stop her from singing, but they couldn't stop her from loving the Lord.

Sudhamani was also given the job of taking her cousins across the backwaters to school. While the children sat in the narrow, wooden boat, Sudhamani stood at the stern, punting the boat across the water with a long bamboo pole.

Because she would suddenly, without warning, slip into a state of total absorption in God, Sudhamani was sometimes caught in dangerous situations.

One day the little one had just finished her job of husking rice paddy, and had a free moment to herself. She got into a little boat and started rowing along the backwaters, greatly enjoying the natural beauty around her. The little waves around the boat sparkled like pure silver, and the sky was covered with a mass of blue-grey clouds. Seeing the clouds filled her with joy because, as usual, their colour reminded her of her Sweet Lord. Suddenly, her mind became totally absorbed in him. The whole sky was filled with Krishna. She completely forgot that she was sitting in the boat. She became oblivious to the world around her. She wasn't even aware of herself. Her whole being was filled with an indescribably joy and bliss. The oars fell from her hands. As the little boat moved hither and thither across the water, she sat absolutely still as a statue, lost in bliss.

Suddenly, a large motorboat came charging down the backwaters. It was a passenger boat heading straight towards Sudhamani's little boat! The captain must not have seen Sudhamani's little boat, but some of the passengers did. They screamed and shouted to catch her attention. But Sudhamani was happily lost in the glorious world of Krishna. She couldn't hear anyone, nor could she see the boat – she had no idea what was happening. A group of people who were standing on the shore also tried to warn her. They shouted and threw stones in the water around Sudhamani. But the Lord wasn't going to let anything happen to Sudhamani, whose mind was so totally focused on him. Just before the passenger boat was about to collide with Sudhamani's little boat and smash it to pieces, she suddenly became aware of her surroundings. She vaguely understood that she was in a dangerous situation. At the last moment she managed to move her boat away so that the big boat just missed her.

When Sudhamani had worked for one year at her aunt's house, she was sent to work for her mother's older brother and his wife. To begin with, they were pleased with Sudhamani because she worked very hard and did everything perfectly.

Several poor Muslim families lived in the area. Many of them didn't have enough food to feed their children. Sudhamani couldn't bear to see them suffer, so she took whatever extra food, clothing and other things she could find in her uncle's house and gave them secretly to those in need. When her aunt and uncle found out what she had done, they beat her severely. From then on, they disliked Sudhamani and were very cruel to her. In the end, Sudhamani decided that she'd had enough, and she left them and went home.

All her other relatives soon learned of her habit of taking food and clothes to give to the poor. Many of them feared that she would come to their homes and give away their belongings as well. From then on, her relatives didn't want to have anything to do with her. She wasn't allowed to put her foot inside their homes. So Sudhamani no longer had to work for her relatives.

Chapter four

Longing for Krishna

Sudhamani was sixteen years old when she returned home. She again took over all the household chores – singing to the Lord and repeating his name over and over as she worked. She also meditated during every spare moment. Because of her intense devotion and her longing for God, tears often streamed down her face as she worked.

Damayanti was deeply embarrassed about her daughter's bad reputation among their relatives. Because of this she treated her even worse than she had before, no matter how perfectly Sudhamani did her work.

Sudhamani had very few clothes. Her sisters and brothers had lots of fine clothes, but she was rarely given anything. One day someone gave her a chequered blouse and she happily put it on. When her brother, Subhagan, saw that she was wearing a new blouse, he immediately ordered her to take it off. He then grabbed the blouse and set it on fire, right in front of her. He shouted at her, "You're wearing these colourful things just because you want to get attention!"

One day Damayanti punished Sudhamani because she had borrowed her sister's yellow jacket. Sudhamani decided that from then on she would wear only the clothes that God gave her. In other words, she would only wear the old, worn-out clothes that had been thrown away by people who didn't want them anymore. The clothes she found were torn and had holes in them. She somehow managed to mend them, using the loose threads from an old clothes line.

Subhagan wouldn't let Sudhamani have anything to do with girls of her own age, because he thought they might be a bad influence on her. When Sudhamani went to fetch drinking water at the village well, she didn't dare speak to any of the village girls, because if Subhagan found out, he would beat her terribly when she came home. So, even though she was now a teenager, she was only allowed to play with small children. But Sudhamani was quite happy about this because she adored children, and when she wasn't with them she preferred to be alone with the Lord.

Sudhamani had a very loving, affectionate nature, and because of this she was always surrounded by children. They felt drawn to her as if she were a magnet. Whenever the children got a chance, they came running to play with her. And they happily followed her when she went to collect leaves for the goats. When Sudhamani climbed up into a tree and sat on a branch to pick the leaves, without even thinking about it she would start making the sound of a flute – Krishna's flute. She felt that she herself was Krishna, and that all the girls and boys were the *gopis* and *gopas*, the milkmaids and cowherd boys of Vrindavan. When she had finished her work she liked to play with her little friends. Together they acted out scenes from Krishna's childhood, and they sang her songs to the Lord. There was a strong bond of love between Sudhamani and the children. The children couldn't keep away from her. They felt so happy in her presence.

Sudhamani noticed that a few of her neighbours earned a living as seamstresses. An idea came to her and she decided that she wanted to take sewing lessons. She thought that if she learned how to sew, she could earn enough money to help the poor. At first her parents wouldn't hear of it, but Sudhamani refused to give up. She kept asking them until they finally relented. So, for a few hours every day, she went to a sewing school that was run by a nearby church. The lessons were held in a little workshop next to the church. While the other girls in the class sat gossiping among themselves about boys, movie stars and the latest fashion, Sudhamani sat by herself, sewing and singing songs to her beloved Krishna. She sang with so much feeling that her tears often fell onto the sewing machine. Although the priest was a Christian, he was deeply moved by Sudhamani's devotion to her Lord, and she became very dear to him.

Sometimes Sudhamani took her embroidery and went out to sit in the graveyard. It was so quiet and peaceful there. She talked to the departed souls, asking them if they were happy, and she sang sacred songs to them so that their souls would rest in peace. Now and then she went inside the church and stood looking at a statue of Jesus Christ being crucified on the cross. The sight of the statue moved her deeply. One day, as she stood gazing at it, she felt that Christ and Krishna were one and the same, and she went into a state of *samadhi*. When she became aware of her surroundings again, she thought about the tremendous self-sacrifice of both Jesus Christ and Krishna, and she thought about their extraordinary love. She burst into tears, thinking, "How they sacrificed everything for the sake of the world! People turned against them, and yet they loved those who hated them. If they could do this, surely I can do it too."

Sudhamani was a good student and quickly learned how to sew. When she left the school, the priest felt so sad that he wept.

He said to her little brother, Satheesh, "Sudhamani will become great in the future. You will see."

Soon Sudhamani started sewing for the villagers. She used the little money she earned to help the poor.

Sometimes at night Sudhamani went outside to look up at the moon and the stars. She said, "O my friends, have you seen my Krishna? Gentle wind, have you ever caressed him? O silent moon and glittering stars, are you also looking for Krishna? If you happen to find him, please tell him that I'm waiting for him. I want to see him!"

Day and night she meditated on the Lord; she sang to him, prayed to him and said his name repeatedly. Her mind never left her Beloved even for a moment.

At last, the day came when Krishna appeared to her. First he appeared as the mischievous, adorable baby Krishna, or Kanna as the baby Krishna is called. Then she saw him when he was a little older, as Gopala, the Divine Cowherd Boy, with a peacock feather in his hair and the flute in his hand. Finally, she saw the Glorious Krishna – the Lord of her heart. Sudhamani was intoxicated with joy. She locked herself in the *puja* room and danced for hours in the sweet bliss of God-consciousness.

From then on, Sudhamani experienced many wonderful visions of Krishna. Whenever she went for a walk, she saw the Lord walking beside her; and he often appeared to her late at night. He teased her in his sweet, mischievous way and made her laugh. The Divine Flute Player took hold of her hands and danced with her on a carpet of fragrant flower petals. He carried her high above the clouds and showed her different worlds and many wonderful things.

Sudhamani was now experiencing that everything in nature was Krishna. Whenever it rained, the raindrops seemed to make the sound, "Om," and she happily sang to the music of the falling rain. She saw Krishna inside each raindrop. She couldn't bring herself to pick a single flower, because every flower was Krishna, and she didn't want to hurt him. When the wind blew, she felt that Krishna was caressing her. When she walked, the ground was Krishna – every grain of sand was he. But she also experienced more and more that there was no difference between Krishna and herself.

It is said that you become what you think about – and so, because Sudhamani's love and longing for Krishna was so intense, and because her mind was always on him, she gradually turned into Krishna himself. She merged with him. But for some time, nobody knew about it. Although outwardly she looked like the same village girl as before – she was small and slim, with long wavy black hair, and a beautiful face with eyes that were unusually radiant and shone with love – inwardly, she had become one with the Lord.

Chapter five

Krishna Bhava

When Sudhamani was later asked how she could attain the state of Self-realization at such a young age, she replied, "From the time I was a small child, I loved the name of God with all my heart. I loved it so much that I would say Krishna's name with every breath I took, over and over again. No matter where I was, or what I was doing, my mind was always on the Lord. For anyone who wants to reach the state of Self-realization, it would help them greatly if they were to think about God all the time, without a moment's interruption."

By now Sudhamani was so close to Krishna that if she just happened to hear the name, "Krishna," her mind immediately became so absorbed in her union with him that she forgot everything else. She spent as much time as possible alone, enjoying her oneness with the Lord. One day Krishna spoke to her. He said, "Thousands upon thousands of people are suffering in this world. You and I are One. Through you I will do much work." It was soon after this that Sudhamani revealed her oneness with Krishna to the world. This is how it happened:

Late one afternoon in September 1975, Sudhamani had just finished picking grass for the cows and was returning home with her brother, Satheesh. She was carrying a big bundle of grass on her head. As usual she was in a divine mood and she sang as she walked. As the two of them passed their neighbours' house, Sudhamani suddenly stopped. The neighbours were sitting in the courtyard. They had been reading about the life of Lord Krishna in the holy scripture, the *Srimad Bhagavatam*, as they did each month. They had just been reading about Lord Krishna's birth and were singing a hymn about him.

Sudhamani stood absolutely still, listening intently to the song. Suddenly her mood changed. The bundle of grass that she was carrying fell to the ground. She ran into the courtyard and stood in the middle of all the people. Her arms were raised and her hands spontaneously formed sacred *mudras*. She was overwhelmed with divine bliss. She couldn't hide her oneness with Krishna anymore. Suddenly, to their great wonder, the people saw that her face had changed. It was Krishna's glorious, radiant face they saw before them. It was the Lord himself who had come among them. Sudhamani was in Krishna *Bhava* – the divine mood of Krishna. Sudhamani asked one of the people to fetch some water. She touched the water and sprinkled it on everyone as holy water.

News about Sudhamani's transformation spread quickly throughout the village and soon a large crowd gathered in the courtyard. But among the people who came to see her, there were some who didn't believe. They thought Sudhamani was just pretending. They said to her, "If you really are Krishna, you should be able to prove it by showing us a miracle. Otherwise, how can we possibly believe in you?"

At first Sudhamani refused. She said to them, "I am not interested in making anyone believe in me by doing miracles. I have no wish to show you any miracles. I want to inspire people to long for God – I want people to long for God-realization. Miracles are not the most important part of spirituality. Besides, if I show you a miracle now, you will soon desire to see another one. You will ask for it again and again. I have not come to the world to create desires; I have come to destroy desires. The real treasure is within you. Why, then, do you want an imitation? Your real Self is within you, but your ignorance hides it."

But the sceptics wouldn't give up. They said, "We promise we won't ask you to do it again."

Finally, Sudhamani agreed. She said, "I will do it just this once, to make you believe. But you must never again come to me with such a wish. Those of you who doubt can come here the next time the Srimad Bhagavatam is being read."

The next time the neighbours had a reading of the Srimad Bhagavatam, a large crowd gathered in their courtyard. There were so many people that everyone couldn't fit in, and some had to stand outside the gate. The people who had come were both believers and non-believers. Some of the non-believers even climbed up into the trees and onto the surrounding rooftops. From up there they could see everything that was happening in the courtyard below. They thought they would soon be able to prove that Sudhamani was just pretending and that she wasn't holy at all. They wanted to make a fool of her.

In the neighbours' courtyard, Sudhamani again went into Krishna Bhava. She then asked one of the people who doubted her the most to bring a jug of water. Just as she had done the last time, she sprinkled the water on the people as holy water. Then she asked the same man who had brought the jug to dip his fingers into the water that was still left in the jug. He did so and saw that the water had turned into pure milk! Sudhamani gave everyone a little of the milk as *prasad*, a sacred gift from God.

She then called another man who also did not believe in her, and asked him to dip his fingers into the jug. Lo and behold! The milk that was left in the jug had turned into a sweet pudding called *panchamritam*. When everyone saw what had happened, they finally understood that it really was Lord Krishna who was standing in front of them, and they called out, "Oh God! Oh God!" The *panchamritam* was given to more than a thousand people, and yet, when everyone had received their share, the jug was still full. The sweet smell of the *panchamritam* remained on everyone's hands for many days afterwards. This event had a great effect on many of the villagers. They became convinced that Sudhamani was not an ordinary person. They understood that she was a *mahatma*, a great soul.

Years later, when Sudhamani was speaking about the beginning of the Krishna Bhava, she said, "I was able to know everything about everyone. I was fully aware that I myself was Krishna, not only during Krishna Bhava, but at all other times as well. When I saw the people and became aware of their suffering, I felt so deeply sorry for them. I knew what each person's problems were, without having to be told about it."

From then on, Sudhamani frequently appeared in Krishna Bhava at the seashore. In the beginning when Sudhamani was in Krishna Bhava, she would lie on a branch of a banyan tree that grew beside the beach. The branch she lay on was very thin and fragile, but it never broke because Sudhamani could make herself as light as a feather.

This holy place became like another Vrindavan, the home of Lord Krishna. During every Krishna Bhava all the devotees sat in front of Sudhamani and sang hymns to Krishna as she blessed everyone who came up to her. The atmosphere was filled with divine joy.

The news about the wonderful Krishna Bhava spread quickly. People started coming from far and wide, from all over Kerala and different parts of India, to see Sudhamani. Many people came to her seeking help because they were suffering in some way. Some were sick, some were very poor, or they had other problems. But no matter what their problems were, they all discovered that when they came to Sudhamani, their troubles would mysteriously disappear. The people who came to her worshipped and adored her, but she herself was so humble that she never for a moment thought she was great in any way.

On the days when there was no Krishna Bhava, Sudhamani continued to work at home and to look after her family. But it was becoming increasingly difficult for her to work because she was often lost in a state of bliss.

Sudhamani's parents decided it was time for their daughter to get married. But Sudhamani refused. She had no intention of getting married. Her parents tried to introduce her to several young men, but she would have nothing to do with them. Whenever her parents brought a possible bridegroom to the house, Sudhamani pretended that she was crazy; she screamed and shouted and tried to look as threatening as possible until the young man and his family became so scared that they ran away. Her parents finally went to an astrologer who knew nothing about Sudhamani. He looked at her horoscope and told them that their daughter was a divine soul, and that they should never even think of getting her married. So her parents gave up the idea of trying to find her a husband.

Chapter six

The Miracles of Sudhamani

Once, when a large crowd had come to the banyan tree for Krishna Bhava, it suddenly began to rain. There was no shelter nearby where the people could protect themselves from the heavy downpour, so they continued to stand beside the tree, expecting to be completely drenched. But to their great wonder they discovered that although it was pouring with rain all around them, not a drop of rain fell on the spot where they were standing!

There was a poisonous cobra on the beach that was frightening people, especially at night. The villagers often saw the snake, and everyone was afraid to walk on the beach after dark. Some of the villagers went up to Sudhamani during Krishna Bhava and asked her to help them.

One evening, during Krishna Bhava, the cobra suddenly appeared beside the banyan tree. When the people saw the snake they ran away and stood at a safe distance. But Sudhamani showed no sign of fear. She caught hold of the cobra, held it up in front of her face and began to touch the snake's flickering tongue with her own tongue! She then let the snake go. It slithered away, and the villagers never saw it again.

It once happened that the children of Mother Sea, as the fishermen were called, were going hungry because they hadn't caught any fish for several days. They came to Sudhamani during Krishna Bhava and told her about their problem. Sudhamani took pity on them. A few days later, she danced on the beach in a state of bliss. To the great joy of the fishermen, a vast school of fish came swimming right up to the shore. Never before in the history of the village had the fishermen caught as many fish as they did that day. It happened three times that Sudhamani called the fish to the shore when the fishermen came to her for help. After that she stopped helping them in this way, because she wanted them to feel real devotion towards God, and not just pray when they needed fish.

What did Sudhamani's parents think of all this? They allowed their daughter to continue the Krishna Bhava, because they believed that Krishna really did come to her at that time and became part of her. But they thought it happened only during Krishna Bhava, and that otherwise she was just a crazy girl. They refused to believe that Sudhamani was one with Krishna at every moment, or that Sudhamani was a great soul.

Sugunanandan didn't like it that the Krishna Bhava was being held on the beach, right next to the road. He felt it wasn't proper for his daughter to be in such a place, where all sorts of people came and went along the road. One night, during Krishna Bhava, he was very upset about this. Sudhamani said to him, "In that case, give me another place where I can receive my devotees. If there is no other place, the cowshed will do." Her father liked the idea and happily agreed.

Sugunanandan rebuilt the cowshed. He made a floor of cement and divided the cowshed into two sections. The two parts were divided in the middle by a wall, which reached only halfway up to the ceiling. The cows lived on one side, and on the other side, a little temple was built for Sudhamani. When you were standing in the temple, you could see the cows on the other side of the low wall. To make it really nice, the walls of the temple were covered with plaited palm leaves.

Sudhamani now began holding Krishna Bhava in the little temple. The devotees brought her a beautiful silver crown with a peacock feather – Krishna's crown – which they wanted her to wear. During her divine mood, Sudhamani would stand in the temple with one foot resting on a small stool, while the people came inside the temple, one after the other, to be blessed by her. Sudhamani's face glowed with divine power. She was just like the mischievous Krishna with an irresistibly sweet twinkle in her eye. She often teased people and made them laugh. Everyone felt so joyful in her presence. As she stood there giving *darshan*[3] to everyone, she often stretched her arm over the low wall and rested her hand on the warm back of one of the cows standing on the other side.

Subhagan hated the new temple. He couldn't stand his sister's strange Krishna Bhava. He burned with anger when he saw how people came to her and how they adored her.

There was an oil lamp[4] in the little temple that was always lit during Krishna Bhava. One day Subhagan broke the oil lamp and poured out all the oil that was used for the lamp. Just before the next Krishna Bhava, some of the devotees went into the

---

[3] *Darshan* is to see or be in the presence of a holy being.
[4] It is a tradition in Hindu temples and homes to light an oil lamp before the altar. This practice, which is carried out during any spiritual activity, signifies the dispelling of darkness.

temple and discovered the broken oil lamp lying on the floor. It was the only lamp they had. When Sudhamani came into the temple and saw how upset they were, she asked them to go to the beach and fetch a few sea shells. She was going to use the shells as oil lamps. But there was no more oil, and you cannot light an oil lamp without any oil. Sudhamani asked the devotees to fill the shells with water, and then to put wicks in the water-filled shells and light them. They did as she told them – and a miracle happened. The "oil lamps" burned brightly, and they continued to burn throughout the night, even though the shells were filled with water instead of oil!

A few days later, a devotee, who didn't know what had happened, brought two new oil lamps which he gave to Sudhamani. He said he had had a dream, and in the dream someone had told him to buy two oil lamps as a gift for Sudhamani.

On the nights when there was no Krishna Bhava, Sudhamani sat outside and meditated under the star-filled sky. Ever since she was a child, she had loved the quietness of the night. Then she could be alone in her divine state, and she could meditate and dance in bliss, without anyone being there to see her.

But there were some villagers who didn't believe in God, and who were against Sudhamani. Her father was afraid that they would come and hurt her one night when she was sitting alone outside in meditation. He became increasingly worried until, finally, he said to her, "Daughter, at night you should come inside and sleep in the house!" But Sudhamani said, "Father, I do not have a home. I prefer to sleep outside. God is everywhere. He is within me and everywhere around me. So there is nothing to worry about. If anyone tries to hurt me, God will protect me."

Chapter seven

The Divine Mother's Child

One day Sudhamani was sitting by herself at home. Her eyes were open but she wasn't looking at anything in the room. She was meditating on the Supreme Truth. Suddenly a ball of brilliant red light appeared in front of her. It was the colour of the most glorious sunset, except that it was much brighter. But though the light was so bright, it was as soft and gentle as moonlight. In front of this wonderful light the Divine Mother appeared to Sudhamani. The Divine Mother was more beautiful than anyone she had ever seen. She wore a shining crown on her head. She looked at Sudhamani with infinite love and smiled at her. Then, just as suddenly as she had come, she was gone. This wonderful vision made Sudhamani so excited that she cried out, "O Krishna, my Mother has come! Please take me to her! I want to hug her so much!" At that moment Krishna came to Sudhamani. He lifted her up and carried her to different worlds. Sudhamani saw strange and wonderful things – but she couldn't see the Divine Mother anywhere. She called out like a small child, "I want to see my Mother! Where is my Mother?" and when she couldn't find her, she began to cry.

After this experience, Sudhamani was in a state of ecstasy for a long time. She felt an intense longing to see the Divine Mother again. She wanted to see her Mother's beautiful face and loving smile. The Divine Mother's love was indescribable and she radiated a light so glorious that it astonished Sudhamani. From then on, Sudhamani could think of nothing but her Mother. Her heart was rushing after the Divine Mother.

Sudhamani's Krishna Bhava continued in the little temple, but apart from that, she spent every moment meditating on the Divine Mother. Day and night, her heart was on fire with longing.

Until now, Sudhamani had continued to help with the household work on the days between the Krishna Bhavas. But now her mind was so concentrated on the Divine Mother that she could no longer do any ordinary work. She could hardly take care of herself at all. She couldn't even eat. For many months she lived on nothing but tulasi leaves[5] and water.

Just as Sudhamani had earlier felt that Krishna was everywhere, she now felt that the Divine Mother was everywhere around her. The whole earth was her Mother, and the wind was her Mother's breath. She roamed about and talked to the trees, the flowers, the birds and the animals. She lay on the ground and rolled around like a small child, calling, "Mother! Mother! Where are you? But, Mother, you are everywhere, so where are you not?"

One day Sudhamani was in the temple and had just finished her meditation. Suddenly she was overwhelmed by a feeling that all of nature was her own Mother and that she herself was a tiny infant – the Divine Mother's child. She crawled out of the temple like a baby and went up to a coconut palm. Sitting close to the

---

[5] The tulasi plant, which is related to basil, is considered sacred.

50

tree, she started crying, "Mother! Mother! Why are you hiding from me? I know that you are hiding in this tree. You are in all the flowers and the plants. You are in the birds and the animals. The whole world is you. Oh Mother, I know that you are hiding in the waves of the ocean and in the wind! Mother, I can't find you!" Suddenly, she felt that her beloved Mother was right there with her. She curled up against her Mother and hugged her close. Sudhamani didn't know that she was hugging the palm tree.

Sudhamani sometimes lay on the ground, looking up at the sky. Dark storm clouds no longer reminded her of Krishna. When she looked at the clouds, she saw her Mother's long, curly hair billowing through the sky. And on a clear day, the sun was her Mother's beautiful, radiant light. Everything in the sky reminded her of the Divine Mother. Sometimes at night, when she lay on the ground looking up at the vast sky filled with moonlight and glittering stars, she felt that the whole sky was her Mother. When she lay on the ground, she never slept; she was praying and crying for her Mother. Tears constantly streamed down her face. She wanted to merge with her Mother. She longed to melt into her, just as a raindrop that falls into the ocean becomes one with the ocean.

Sudhamani had a *mantra*[6] which she repeated again and again. No guru had given her this *mantra*. She had made it up herself. Her *mantra* was "Amma, Amma, Amma…" (Mother, Mother, Mother…). She never took a single step without saying her *mantra*. If she ever forgot to say it when she took a step, she immediately took a step back and said, "Amma." Only then would she allow herself to continue. Sometimes Sudhamani went

---

[6] A mantra is either God's name or a few sacred words that you say over and over, day after day, no matter what you are doing. If you keep saying the mantra, the spiritual power that you have within you will awaken and you will become one with God.

swimming in the backwaters. Before she dived into the water, she would decide how many times she had to say her *mantra* before coming back up to the surface. If a moment happened to pass without her remembering the Divine Mother, she felt deeply troubled and confessed, "Mother, I have wasted so much time!" To make up for the lost time, she would meditate longer than usual that day. If she happened to miss a meditation, she would spend the whole night outside, walking back and forth, saying her *mantra* and praying, "Mother, what is the use of this life if I can't meditate on you? O Mother, give me strength! Let me see you! Let me merge with you!"

If someone came up to her and started talking to her, she imagined it was the Divine Mother standing in front of her. The person would go on talking until he or she realized that Sudhamani had mysteriously slipped off into another world.

In the mornings, when she started brushing her teeth, she often couldn't finish her task because her mind would suddenly fly towards the Divine Mother, and she would completely forget what she was doing. It could then take hours before she became aware of her surroundings again. It was even more difficult for her to take a bath. When she entered the bathroom, she usually discovered that she had forgotten her towel. And when she had fetched the towel, she noticed that she had also forgotten her soap or something else. Then she thought, "Mother, I'm wasting all this time just trying to take a bath! Let my mind always be on you instead. I feel so sad when I forget you even for a second." She would then decide to forget about her bath. Instead she'd sit down on the bathroom floor, and soon she was in a state of deep meditation. Hours later, someone in the family would find her sitting there. To make her come out of her meditation, they poured a bucket of cold water over her head. In this way she finally got a bath after all! If pouring water on her didn't help, they shook her very hard. Sometimes, they had to carry her out of the bathroom.

Most of all, Sudhamani liked to go down to the beach and meditate beside the ocean in the middle of the night, when everything was quiet and peaceful. The waves breaking against the shore were singing their endless song, "Om... Om... Om." The dark-blue sky was sparkling with millions of twinkling stars. Everything reminded Sudhamani of her Divine Mother. It took her only a moment to slip into a deep state of meditation, her mind resting contentedly in the lap of the Beautiful Mother of the Universe.

On such a night, if her father happened to be looking for her, he would get very worried when he couldn't find her in the house or anywhere outside. Eventually, he would go down to the beach to look for her. There he usually found her in deep meditation, sitting absolutely still like a rock.

Unable to understand her, Sudhamani's family continued to believe that she was just a crazy girl. But she was really in a state of supreme devotion. She longed for the Divine Mother just as a person who is held under water longs for air. She loved the Divine Mother more than her own life.

Subhagan was still treating Sudhamani very badly. One day, as she was walking into the house, he stopped her at the door and shouted, "I forbid you to enter this house! Only when you stop all your shameful dancing and singing, will I allow you to come inside again." Because Sudhamani thought that everything that happened to her was the Divine Mother's will, she thought this must also be her will. So she left the house without saying a word and sat down in the courtyard in front of the house. But Subhagan ordered her not to sit there either. Sudhamani then took a handful of sand and gave it to her brother, saying, "If this sand belongs to you, please tell me how many grains of sand there are."

From then on she lived outside by herself.

Day and night, she continued to long for the Divine Mother. Nothing else mattered to her. Like a little child, with tears streaming down her face, she stretched out her arms towards the sky, as if she were reaching for her Mother. She cried and she begged her Mother to come to her. "Oh Mother," she cried, "where are you? Have you left me here to die of longing? You are my only hope. Have you abandoned me just like everyone else? Can't you see how much I'm suffering?"

When the children in the neighbourhood saw her crying, they came to her and asked, "Elder sister, why are you crying? Do you have pain somewhere?" They sat close to her, and because they loved her so much and couldn't bear to see her so sad, they also began to cry. Finally, they figured out the reason why Sudhamani was crying: it was because she wanted to see the Divine Mother. So the little girls put on saris and came to her, pretending that they were the Divine Mother. Sudhamani hugged them when she saw them dressed like that. She didn't think of them as children; to her, they were the Divine Mother herself.

Sudhamani's longing for the Divine Mother became so strong that she could no longer think about anything else. She didn't take care of herself or notice anything around her. She no longer knew the difference between day and night. She lay on the ground in a state of deep meditation. She didn't notice when the sun was burning hot or when it poured with rain. She didn't sleep and she never thought about food.

Just as Sudhamani was sometimes in Krishna Bhava, she was now in the Bhava [mood] of a two-year-old child, the Divine Mother's Child. Sudhamani cried like a small child for her Mother. At other times she laughed and clapped her hands. She rolled on the ground and tried to hug the earth; she went to the backwaters and tried to kiss the ripples on the water. All the time she was calling out, "Mother! Mother!"

One day some devotees came to visit Sudhamani. They found her lying on the ground near the backwaters, unconscious of the world around her. Her mind was totally absorbed in the Divine Mother. Her face and hair were full of sand, and there were tracks of the never-ending tears on her cheeks. The devotees were heartbroken when they saw her lying there. They went and told her father, but Sugunanandan didn't want to hear about it. It made them very sad to think that no one in her family cared about her. They carried her into the house and laid her on a bed, not knowing that it was Subhagan's bed. They cleaned her and tried in vain to bring her back to external consciousness. Then they left her there to rest comfortably.

When Subhagan came home a little later and found his sister lying on his bed, he flew into a fit of rage and screamed, "Who put this wretch on my bed!" He shook the bed with such force that it broke into pieces. But Sudhamani didn't notice a thing. She just lay there peacefully in the middle of the rubble. Later when Sudhamani found out what had happened, she didn't react at all. She simply said, "Whatever happens is God's will, and it is always for the best."

The next day a devotee, who was a carpenter, and who knew nothing about what had happened the day before, came to Sudhamani with a bed, a table and a few chairs. He told her that he had had a dream in which Lord Krishna appeared to him and commanded him to bring the furniture as a gift for Sudhamani.

Faithful Friends

Des amis fidèles

Wild birds and animals felt very drawn to Sudhamani. They could sense her love towards all of God's creatures, from the smallest ant to a human being. Even the shyest animals instinctively trusted her and weren't afraid of her at all.

Now, when Sudhamani was living outside, it was the animals who looked after her and befriended her. Her family had more or less abandoned her and were against her spiritual life, but the animals adored her and did their best to make her as happy and comfortable as possible. No matter what the weather, they always stayed close to her and protected her. The animals seemed to understand her much better than any human being ever had.

Sudhamani liked to meditate in the little temple every day. Whenever she came out of the temple, one of the cows belonging to the family came up to her, wanting to feed her with its own milk. Sudhamani thought the Divine Mother must have arranged this. So she drank the milk directly from the cow's udder, like a baby calf. Thanks to the cow, she didn't have to go hungry or thirsty. The cow loved Sudhamani so much that it refused to eat any grass or to feed its own calf before it had given Sudhamani her daily milk. This irritated Sudhamani's family. The cow used to go to the temple every day and stand there, waiting patiently for Sudhamani. Sudhamani's parents tried several times to move the cow away from the temple, but the cow wouldn't budge. They even pulled the animal by its tail and poured buckets of water over it, but no matter how they tried, it wouldn't move an inch. Sometimes the cow became spirited and ran playfully around the palm trees with the angry family chasing after it. But they couldn't catch it. Then it would run back to Sudhamani to feed her. And as soon as Sudhamani had been given her milk, the cow was more than willing to be led away.

Sudhamani's uncle lived close to her grandmother's house. One day he noticed that one of his cows had escaped and was running towards the ocean. At the beach, the cow made a sharp turn to the right and began trotting at full speed along the seashore, with Sudhamani's uncle chasing it. The cow was running so fast that he couldn't catch it. Finally it turned inland and ran straight towards Parayakadavu, where it had never been before. The cow went straight to the Idammanel property, where Sudhamani was sitting outside, absorbed in meditation. The cow walked up to her, gently caressed Sudhamani with its soft nose and licked her. But Sudhamani was in deep meditation and didn't notice anything. The cow then lay down nearby and looked intently at Sudhamani, as if waiting for her to come out of her meditation. After a while, Sudhamani opened her eyes, and as soon as she saw the cow, she got up and walked over to the animal. At that moment the cow raised one of its hind legs, inviting Sudhamani to drink its milk. Sudhamani was very thirsty and happily drank from the cow. Her uncle, who had been watching the whole scene, was filled with wonder. That day he understood that Sudhamani was not an ordinary soul.

The cow went to visit Sudhamani several times, each time offering Sudhamani its milk.

Even snakes were drawn to Sudhamani. It happened many times that a snake came and coiled itself around her body when she was sitting outside absorbed in deep meditation. Even poisonous snakes came to her, but they were always friendly and never harmed her. They just wanted to be near her.

Wild birds were completely tame in Sudhamani's presence. She especially loved the wild parrots, because it was said that they had a special relationship with the Divine Mother. Sometimes when she prayed, "O Mother, won't you come to me?" a flock of parrots came flying through the air and settled on the ground next to her. One day a devotee gave Sudhamani a caged parrot as a present. But Sudhamani couldn't bear the thought of keeping any living creature in a cage, so she set the parrot free. But the bird didn't fly away. He chose to stay with Sudhamani. People often saw the parrot playing around her. It looked as if he was dancing. One day when Sudhamani was praying to the Divine Mother she began to cry. Suddenly she looked up and saw the parrot standing in front of her. The parrot was crying as well. The bird could feel Sudhamani's sadness, and it made him sad too.

Apart from the parrot, two pigeons also liked to be close to Sudhamani. Whenever she sang to the Divine Mother, the two pigeons and the parrot came and stood in front of her. As she sang her song, they danced merrily, spreading out their wings and hopping about.

High up in a palm tree near the house was an eagle's nest with two baby birds. One day the nest was disturbed and fell to the ground in pieces. The two eaglets lay helpless on the ground. Some children began throwing stones at the baby birds and tried to kill them. At that moment Sudhamani arrived on the scene and saved them. She made a little shelter for the birds and nursed them carefully. A few weeks later the eaglets were strong enough to begin to fly, and Sudhamani set them free. For a long time the two eagles used to appear at the beginning of each Krishna Bhava, perched on the roof of the temple.

The eagle, Garuda, is said to be the vehicle of the Lord. So now, Sudhamani had *two* Garudas during Krishna Bhava. The devotees loved the eagles and eagerly looked for them at the beginning of every Krishna Bhava.

Sudhamani often cried so much for the Divine Mother that she lost all external consciousness. Whenever this happened, the two Garudas came flying and landed right next to her. They stood watching over her, as if they were protecting her. One day some women from the neighbourhood came walking by and saw Sudhamani lying unconscious on the ground with the two Garudas standing close to her, gazing at her face. The women were amazed to see that the eagles were weeping like human beings. The two eagles loved Sudhamani so much that they couldn't bear to see her suffer.

Another day, when she had just finished meditating, Sudhamani felt very hungry. One of the eagles immediately flew towards the ocean and came back a few minutes later with a fish gripped in its claws. It gently dropped the fish onto her lap. Sudhamani was so hungry that she picked up the fish and ate it raw. From then on the eagle caught a fish for her every day. Damayanti soon found out about this. She didn't like the idea of her daughter eating raw fish, so whenever she saw the eagle arrive with its daily offering, she'd grab the fish and fry it for her daughter. Before this, when Sudhamani used to worship Krishna, she never ate any fish. But now, she was convinced that the Divine Mother herself was sending the eagle to catch the fish for her. As far as Sudhamani was concerned, the fish was sacred food that was given to her by the

Goddess, and so she ate it. The eagle continued to catch fish for Sudhamani for a long time.

A cat also came to stay with her. The cat used to enter the temple during Krishna Bhava and walk in a perfect circle around Sudhamani, just as people walk in a circle around the images of the gods and goddesses in Hindu temples. The cat then sat down next to her, totally unconcerned about all the people in the temple. It sat there for a long time, with its eyes closed. Everyone believed the cat was meditating. One day someone tried to get rid of the cat by taking it across the backwaters and leaving it there, but the very next day the cat came back; it probably swam. It continued to stay close to Sudhamani.

A big black and white dog was Sudhamani's loyal friend. The dog adored her. Whenever Sudhamani cried for the Divine Mother with such intensity that she lost all external consciousness, the dog was heartbroken and began to whine loudly. He rubbed himself against her and licked her face, trying to make her wake up. And whenever she had to cross the backwaters to go somewhere, the dog got very upset. He barked loudly in protest and tried to stop her from leaving by pulling at her skirt.

Now and then the dog came to her with a food packet in his mouth, which he lay at her feet. No one knew where the packet came from, and the dog never ate a grain of rice from the food. At night he slept close beside her. When Sudhamani would lie down on the ground to gaze at the sky, she would rest her head on the dog's back, using him as a pillow.

Whenever a devotee bowed down before Sudhamani, as a mark of respect, the black and white dog liked to stretch out his front legs and bend his head down, as if he, too, were bowing down before her. And when Sudhamani danced in a state of devotional ecstasy, the dog jumped happily up and down around her, as if he were dancing as well. Whenever the sacred conch was blown in the temple, the dog howled, managing to sound almost exactly like the conch.

One night Sudhamani was meditating on the banks of the backwaters, when her father happened to walk by. Sudhamani was sitting absolutely still. She was in such a deep state of meditation that she didn't notice that her body was covered by a thick blanket of mosquitoes. Her father kept calling her, trying to bring her out of her meditation; but her mind was far away and she couldn't hear him. He then began to shake her violently, as was the usual custom of the family. But no matter how hard he shook her, he couldn't bring her back. As he shook her, he discovered to his surprise that she seemed to weigh no more than a small twig. He sat down beside her. A moment later, the black and white dog came up to Sudhamani and barked at her, as if trying to get her attention. A few minutes later, Sudhamani opened her eyes and was back to normal. It was as if the animals could always get her attention, no matter what world she was in.

The dog loved Sudhamani so much that she sometimes thought the dog was the Divine Mother herself. When this happened Sudhamani felt just like a small child. She hugged and kissed the dog and called out, "Mother! Mother!"

One day when Sudhamani was meditating, she suddenly felt extremely restless. She stood up and walked quickly to the village. Her dog had been caught by a dog catcher, who was about to take it away to be killed. The dog was whining loudly, unable to escape from the dog catcher's chain. As the man took him away, the dog dragged his paws on the ground. A few of the village girls who were very fond of Sudhamani recognized the dog and came running. They explained to the man that the dog belonged to their friend, and they begged him to let it go, but the man ignored them. They even offered him some money. Just then Sudhamani arrived. The dog looked pitifully at Sudhamani and began shedding tears like a human being! This was too much for the dog catcher. He could clearly see how much the dog loved her, and so he had no choice but to set him free. The dog was caught a few more times by different dog catchers, but Sudhamani always managed to save him at the last moment.

One day Sudhamani had a strong feeling that her friend, the black and white dog, was about to get sick and die. A few days later, this is exactly what happened. The dog became infected with rabies. But he hardly suffered at all. When Sudhamani was asked if she was sad that her dog had died, she said, "I am not sad at all, because even though he has died, he will soon come back to me." Some time later she said that the soul of the dog had been born again nearby. But she wouldn't say anything more about it.

A person who is one with God loves all of God's creatures – every one of them without exception – because he or she can clearly see God in everyone. When your heart is filled with divine love and compassion, animals feel drawn to you as if you were a magnet. Wild lions and tigers become like meek little lambs in your presence, and poisonous snakes would never dream of harming you. All of God's creatures become your dear friends. This is what happened to Sudhamani. Sudhamani could even understand the language of the animals. When they spoke to her, she understood everything they said.

Chapter nine

Mother of Sweet Bliss

Sudhamani now felt the Divine Mother's presence all around her, and she could sense her Beloved Mother wherever she looked. She hugged the trees and stroked the flowers, because she felt they were her Mother. She talked to them and kissed them. When the wind blew on her hair and her skin, she felt that the Divine Mother was caressing her. The earth was her Mother's lap. She rolled on the ground trying to hug the earth. She often gazed at the sky with a faraway look on her face. No one knew what she was seeing. She would suddenly be filled with such bliss that she laughed and cried at the same time, without being able to stop.

Because Sudhamani's mind was always on the Divine Mother, she didn't sleep and she hardly ever ate. She could no longer take care of her own body because her mind was in another world. Sometimes, when she did eat, she'd end up eating used tea leaves, cow dung or other strange things, because she couldn't tell the difference. She had no idea what she was eating. An ordinary person couldn't eat such things without getting sick, but because of Sudhamani's divine state, it didn't hurt her at all.

Sudhamani's devotion towards the Divine Mother reached its highest peak. Her longing to see her Mother was so strong that she often cried for hours on end, until she couldn't bear it anymore and reached a point where she lost all outer consciousness.

One day she felt so sad that she cried out, "O Mother, I can't bear the pain of being separated from you! Why don't you come to me? I can't live without you!"

Many years later, when she looked back on this moment, she said, "Every pore of my body was wide open with longing; every atom of my body was vibrating with the sacred *mantra* – my whole being was running towards the Divine Mother like a rushing river."

She felt her heart was about to break with longing and she cried out, "O Mother! Your child is longing for you so much! Why don't you come? I'm like a fish being thrown on dry land. Don't you care about me? I have given you everything I have. Now, I have nothing left to give you except my last breath."

Her voice became choked and she collapsed to the ground. If she couldn't have the Divine Mother, there was nothing more to live for. She had offered the Mother everything she had and everything she was – her whole being. And now she was giving the Divine Mother her last breath. Sudhamani stopped breathing. She was about to die.

But then, suddenly, something wonderful happened!

The Mother of the Universe knows everything that happens to her children, and she had no intention of letting Sudhamani die. And so, at this moment, the Divine Mother appeared to her. The Divine Mother was shining like a million suns. Sudhamani's joy knew no bounds. Her heart was overwhelmed by a wave of indescribable love and bliss, and she was lifted to the heights of God-consciousness. Afterwards she wrote a song, trying to describe what it was like. The song is called "The Path of Bliss."

Once upon a time,
My soul was dancing in delight
Along the Path of Bliss.
I found myself in a golden dream,
And my mind was filled
With all that is good and noble.

With gentle shining hands
The Divine Mother caressed me.
I bowed my head and told Mother
That my life belongs to Her.

Lovingly, Mother smiled at me.
She turned into a Divine Light
And melted into me.
My mind blossomed
Shining in every colour of the rainbow.

I could see the whole world
And everything that has ever happened.
I saw that I am part of everything,
And everything is part of me.
I turned away from the meaningless pleasures of the world,
And merged with the Divine Mother.

Mother told me to ask everyone
Never to forget the reason why we are born.
And so, I am telling the whole world—
Especially those who are lost in the dark—
The truth that Mother spoke:
"My Children, come and merge with Me."

Today, I tremble with bliss
As I remember Her words:
"Oh My darling child,
Leave everything else and
Come to Me!
You belong to Me forever."

O Pure Consciousness,
Embodiment of Truth,
I will do exactly as You say.
O Mother, I don't know anything.
If I have made any mistakes
Please forgive me.

Sudhamani had, at last, become one with the Divine Mother. Not only had the drop of water melted into the ocean – the drop had become the ocean itself. There was no longer any difference between Sudhamani and the Divine Mother. Sudhamani was the Divine Mother.

And so, from now on we will call her Mother.

She was aware of herself being everywhere in the whole universe. Later, when she tried to explain the experience to her questioning devotees, she said, "I experienced how the Divine Mother, in all her different forms, exists within myself, and I realized that I am not different or separate from her. At that point, I saw that all of Creation exists within me like a tiny bubble."

Mother now spent her days and nights alone outside, enjoying the sweet bliss of Self-realization.

One day she heard a voice that said, "My child, I am in everyone, and not in one special place. You were not born just to enjoy the state of bliss. You have come to the world to help those who are suffering. From now on, worship me in everyone, and take away their suffering."

From then on, apart from Krishna Bhava, Mother also appeared in Devi Bhava, the mood of the Divine Mother. During Devi Bhava she dressed in a colourful sari and wore a beautiful crown. At this time she allowed people to see more of her oneness with Devi, the Divine Mother.

Her heart overflowed with love and compassion. Just as a mother loves her children, the Holy Mother loved everyone. But her love was infinitely deeper and stronger than the love of any ordinary mother. When people came to her, they knelt before her and she held each one in her arms. Thousands of people began to come to her. She blessed them, comforted them, and took away their suffering.

Chapter ten

Troublemakers

Mother's family still didn't understand her. They thought it was terrible that so many people came to see her. They even thought she was giving the family a bad reputation because she was mixing with so many different people! It was for this reason that her older brother, Subhagan, and some of her cousins decided to kill her. They came to her one day and told her that a relative wanted to see her. So she went with them to the relative's house. But no one was at home. They had been lying to her. Subhagan and her cousins brought her into the house. One of her cousins took out a big knife, which he had been hiding under his clothes. Subhagan said to Mother, "Your behaviour has gone too far! You are giving the family a bad reputation. Because you won't stop singing and dancing and mixing with all kinds of people, it is better that you die!"

Mother laughed at him and said, "I am not afraid of death. Sooner or later the body must come to an end. But it is impossible for you or for anyone else to kill my real Self. If you are going to put an end to this body, I will tell you what my last wish is, and it is your duty to fulfil that wish. I want you to let me meditate for a while, and then, when I am absorbed in meditation, you are free to kill this body."

Mother was perfectly calm. She sat down, closed her eyes and went into a deep state of meditation. Her face shone with bliss. The men were so stunned by her words and by her peaceful, radiant face that they couldn't speak.

Suddenly, the cousin who was holding the knife ran forward and pressed the knife against Mother's chest. But before he could hurt her, he froze and was struck by a terrible pain in his own chest, at the exact spot where he had pressed the knife against Mother. His pain was so great that he collapsed on the floor. When the others saw this, they were terrified.

At that moment Damayanti arrived. She had felt that something was wrong when she saw her daughter leave the house with Subhagan and their cousins, and she had followed them. When she arrived at the house, she guessed that something terrible was happening. She shouted at the top of her voice and banged on the door until it was finally opened. Damayanti grabbed hold of Mother's hand and quickly led her away from the house.

The cousin who had raised the knife against Mother became very sick and had to be hospitalised. Mother visited him at the hospital. She felt no anger towards him – only compassion. She lovingly consoled him and fed him with her own hands. When he experienced Mother's love and forgiveness, he deeply regretted what he had done, and burst into tears. He died a few days later.

Soon thereafter, Subhagan became seriously ill with elephantiasis. But even during his illness he was filled with hatred and threatened Mother's devotees. Not long thereafter, he became very depressed about his illness and committed suicide.

Sugunanandan and Damayanti were heartbroken. But Mother said to them, "Do not be sad, for Subhagan will soon be born again into this family." A few years later, Mother's older sister, Kasturi, got married and had a son called Shivan. Mother told her family that Subhagan had been born again as Shivan. Mother showered the little boy with love. He adored her right from the start and was very close to her. So great was Mother's compassion, that she had saved the soul of her brother who had always been so cruel to her and had tried to harm her.

Some people in the village were atheists and didn't believe in Mother. They were so much against her that they wanted to hurt her. One day they went to a place where Mother often sat for meditation and they threw sharp nails all over the ground. But strangely enough, even though Mother went and sat there, she didn't feel the slightest prick. The atheists then became so angry that a few of them went to her during Krishna Bhava and, pretending to be devotees, they offered her a glass of poisoned milk. Although Mother knew that the milk was poisoned, she accepted it and drank it. The men waited for her to collapse and die. But the poison couldn't harm her. After a few moments Mother turned in their direction, vomited the poisoned milk right in front of them, and continued with the Krishna Bhava as if nothing had happened. The atheists quickly fled from the place.

The hostile villagers now joined a large group of atheists from several neighboring villages and formed a club called the Rationalist Club. Their aim was to harm the Holy Mother. They wanted to make people believe she was a fake, and that she wasn't holy at all. They spread false rumours about her and even wrote bad things about her in the newspapers.

In those days, during Devi Bhava, Mother would come out of the temple in the divine mood of Mother Kali. She would hold the Divine Mother's sword and trident in her hands and dance in a state of rapture. One evening the Rationalists brought a basket full of sharp, poisonous thorns. They gave the basket to a group of children and instructed them to scatter the thorns on the ground where Mother always danced. They told the children to be careful not to touch the thorns. That night, when Mother came out of the temple, she knew what had happened without anyone having told her. She told her devotees about the thorns and asked them not to move from the place where they were standing. Mother then began to dance her divine dance, with the sword and trident in her hands. It was a dance like no other dance they had ever seen. They felt as if Mother Kali herself, the Destroyer of all evil, was dancing before them. She was dancing barefoot on the veranda in front of the temple. Suddenly her sword cut the strings that were holding up some pictures on the wall. The pictures fell with a crash to the ground, scattering broken glass all over the veranda. But Mother took no notice and continued to dance. She danced on the broken glass as if it were soft flower petals.

Then Mother stepped down from the temple veranda and went straight to the place where the thorns had been scattered, and she danced on the poisonous thorns.

The Rationalists who had come to harm her were wonder-struck when they saw her dancing on the thorns. They stood there waiting, expecting her feet to bleed and be covered with thorns. They were sure she was about to collapse from the poison. But nothing happened. Later, when the Devi Bhava was over, her worried father came to her with some medicines to put on her feet. But he discovered that there was not the slightest trace of a scratch or a prick on her feet.

One day the Rationalists sent an evil sorcerer to Mother during Devi Bhava. The sorcerer was famous for his black magic. He had harmed many people in the past, and now he was going to try his deadly sorcery on Mother. He gave her some ash, pretending it was a gift of holy ash. But there was nothing holy about it. It was ordinary ash that he had poisoned with his evil magic. The ash was so powerful that it could easily kill the person who used it. As soon as the sorcerer offered her the ash, Mother knew what it was, but she didn't say anything. She accepted it and rubbed it on herself. She was thinking, "If it is God's will that this body should die from this, let it happen. No one can escape God's will." The man was sure that Mother would die from his evil magic just as many others had died. But to his great surprise nothing happened. Not long thereafter, the black magician went mad and ended his days as a crazy beggar in the streets.

The Rationalists refused to give up. They even hired a murderer, who went into the little temple during Devi Bhava, with a knife hidden under his clothes. As soon as Mother saw him, she smiled at him lovingly. Her smile had a strange effect on him. He fell at her feet begging her to forgive him for what he had intended to do. He walked out of the temple a changed man. Seeing the change in him, the Rationalists insulted him. But he just smiled at them. From then on he was a devotee of Mother.

The Rationalists now went to the police and lied to them about Mother, accusing her of crimes she had never committed. Responding to this, a group of policemen came to Mother one day to question her. Mother laughed when she saw them and said, "Please arrest me if you like and lock me in your jail. At least there I can be alone, and then I can meditate all the time and think about God. If it's God's will, let it be done." She continued to laugh joyfully as she stretched out her hands towards them. The policemen were dumbfounded. When they saw the radiant love and joy on her face, most of them understood that they were standing before a great soul, and they were filled with awe. They prostrated at her feet and felt blessed. The policemen soon left, and they never again had any doubts about Mother. Thus, the Rationalists had once again failed to harm her.

Mother, who knew everything and could see into the future, said that the Rationalist Club would soon come to an end. This is exactly what happened. The members of the club started quarrelling with each other. There were some among them who had a change of heart. They began to believe in Mother and realized they had made a terrible mistake. These people became her devotees, and two of the leaders later married Mother's own sisters. Thus the Rationalist Club came to an end.

When Mother's father had made the little temple for her in the cowshed, he never imagined that thousands of people would come to see her. More and more people were pouring in during Krishna and Devi Bhava, and Sugunanandan was upset about this. He couldn't stand the thought of her mixing with so many strangers. Like the rest of the family, he thought she was giving the family a bad reputation. As far as Sugunanandan was concerned, Mother was just his daughter. He was also worried because after every Devi Bhava, Mother's body became as stiff as a statue. Someone had to massage her for hours to bring her body back to normal.

One evening, when he was feeling particularly worried, he went up to Mother during Devi Bhava. Years earlier she had said to him that only God was her real Father and Mother, and when she was talking to him now, she called him "foster-father." Sugunanandan, who was already in a bad mood because of his worries, almost exploded with anger when she called him that. He shouted at her, "Do gods and goddesses have foster-fathers? Goddess, I want my daughter back!" Mother replied, "If I give your daughter back to you, you will get nothing but a dead body, and you will have to bury her!" Mother meant that Sugunanandan was only the father of her body – he was not the father of her soul. She herself – the eternal Self that could never die – didn't belong to anyone. So if he wanted his daughter back, he could only have the body – nothing else. But Sugunanandan wasn't in the mood to listen. He demanded, "Let the Divine Mother leave and go back to her own place. I want my child back!" Mother said to him, "If that is what you want, here is your daughter. Take her!" Mother collapsed and fell to the floor. Her eyes were still open but she didn't move. Her heart stopped beating and her body stiffened. A doctor happened to be among the devotees. He took Mother's pulse, but there was no sign of life. He gently closed her eyes and pronounced her dead.

The people were devastated. Many of them wept. Others became hysterical with shock. At first Sugunanandan just stood there, completely stunned. He didn't know what to do. Then he realized that it was because of him that his daughter had died. He was so overwhelmed with grief that he collapsed.

Oil lamps were lit around Mother's body. Everyone had given up hope. The people were so heartbroken they couldn't speak. Everything was quiet around the temple. Even Mother Nature was silent. You couldn't hear a single wave breaking against the shore, not a cricket chirped, and the wind stopped rustling in the trees.

Eight hours passed, but no one moved. Everyone sat quietly around Mother's body. Then Sugunanandan stood up and wept aloud. With tears streaming down his face, he cried out, "Divine Mother! I beg you to forgive me! I didn't know what I was saying. Please bring my daughter back to life! Forgive me! I'll never say such things again." As he prayed, he fell to the ground crying uncontrollably.

Suddenly, someone noticed that Mother's body seemed to move a little. Had they imagined it or was she really moving? Slowly Mother opened her eyes and came back to life. She was perfectly strong and healthy, as if nothing had happened. The joy and relief of everyone knew no bounds.

From that day, a great change came over Sugunanandan. He finally understood that his daughter was the Divine Mother herself. From then on, he stopped trying to change her, and allowed her to do whatever she liked.

Chapter eleven

Embracing the world

In 1975, when Mother first revealed her oneness with God in the form of Krishna and Devi, she said to her father, "Do not ask anyone for anything. Everything will come to you, without you having to ask for it. God will bless you and give you whatever you need. In the future, this place will become a great spiritual centre; my devotees will come here from all over the world. Thousands of my devotees will become like your own children and your family to you."

Soon thereafter, the first group of Indian youths left their homes and came to live with Mother. Mother showered the *brahmacharis*[7] with love and treated them as if they were her own children. Under the wing of her loving guidance they began to live a life of renunciation. Their desire to be with her was so intense that they took no notice of the fact that there was hardly any food available. They spent most of their time out in the open, sleeping on the bare ground without even a mat. Whatever they really needed came to them without their having to ask for it, and

---

[7] A brahmachari or a brahmacharini is a spiritual student who is being trained by a guru.

they shared everything among themselves. They had no money. Whenever they had to go somewhere, they walked, even if it was a great distance. They had only one set of clothes each, but they somehow learned to manage.

One day one of the *brahmacharis* was feeling depressed because his only set of clothes was dirty and worn out. He complained to Mother about their poverty. She said to him, "Do not ask God for such small things. Surrender yourself at his feet and he will give you whatever you really need." Mother had lived that way herself, and was therefore speaking from her own experience. The very next day, a devotee who didn't know how very poor they were brought new clothes for all the *brahmacharis*.

Because of the difficult circumstances during those early days at the ashram, the *brahmacharis* received an all-round training in renunciation. To encourage them, Mother used to say, "If you can endure the training you get here, you will be able to feel at home anywhere. If you can overcome these difficult situations, in the future it will be easy for you to cope with any difficulty."

In the early days when Mother's ashram was being formed, one of her disciples gave her the name "Mata Amritanandamayi Devi," and that is the name by which she is known today throughout the world. But most people call her "Amma" which means "Mother."

Mother's family gradually realized that Mother was the Divine Mother herself, and a vast change came over them. Sugunanandan and Damayanti often wondered what good deeds they had done in their past lives to become the "parents" of the Divine Mother!

When Mother was asked why she had been born into such difficult circumstances, being misunderstood, abused and rejected by her own family and many of the villagers, Mother replied that she had chosen to be born into that situation in order to inspire and encourage people. She wanted to show mankind that Self-realization can be attained despite the most difficult circumstances imaginable.

Mother has also stated that she has always been in the same state of supreme consciousness, that she was always, even as a baby, fully aware of her oneness with God. And so it is believed that she went through those early years of longing and striving for oneness with Krishna and the Divine Mother just to set an example for others to follow.

Today, the place where Mother grew up is called Amritapuri. And Mother's home has become an ashram, called the Mata Amritanandamayi Math, where Mother is training hundreds of men and women, who have chosen to dedicate their lives to God and to serve humanity. Thousands of families, both in India and throughout the world, think of the ashram as their spiritual home.

At the ashram, Mother can often be seen working with everyone, carrying bricks and sand, cutting vegetables, etc. When there is a difficult or dirty job to be done, Mother doesn't say to people, "Go and do it." Instead, Mother herself goes and does the work. Soon everyone comes rushing to help, and in no time the job is done.

Mother is always teaching her children by her own example. On one occasion, there was a hole in the roof of one of the huts where the residents were staying, so that when it rained, water leaked into the hut. The two *brahmacharis* who were supposed to mend the roof kept postponing the job. They kept saying, "Let's do it tomorrow instead," and so it never got done. Mother found out about this one morning. She immediately went to the hut, and having asked for a ladder, she climbed up onto the leaking roof and began to fix it. When the *brahmacharis* discovered what Mother was doing, they came running. They pleaded with her to get down from the roof so that they could mend it, but she wouldn't hear of it. Mother mended the roof herself, while the two *brahmacharis* stood watching her, feeling deeply ashamed of themselves. After that, the *brahmacharis* always did the work they were supposed to do, immediately, without postponing it to "another day."

Another time, a sick girl who had come to the ashram vomited on a sari. A *brahmacharini*, who was serving Mother and who used to wash Mother's clothes, felt so disgusted that she picked up the dirty cloth with a stick and was about to hand it over to a washerman. When Mother saw this she said, "If you cannot see God in everyone, and if you cannot serve everyone equally, then what is the use of having done so many years of service and meditation? Is there any difference between Mother and that sick girl?" Mother then took the cloth and washed it herself.

Mother has dedicated every moment of her life, both day and night, to the service of humanity. Because Mother is always thinking about others, she tends to forget about herself and doesn't even notice when she is hungry or thirsty or tired. Every day, hundreds, often thousands, of people come to Mother for *darshan*. They tell her about their problems and Mother listens to them for hours on end. She wipes their tears and eases their suffering. Everyone who comes to Mother gets a hug from her. Throughout the years, Mother has lovingly embraced millions of people. Whether they are young or old, rich or poor, good or bad, she accepts them all with the same extraordinary love and tenderness. Mother is their guide and support; she comforts them and helps them through all their difficulties.

Mother is doing all that she can to help those who are poor and suffering. She has an orphanage near the ashram where her *brahmacharis* and *brahmacharinis* are looking after hundreds of boys and girls who have no parents, or whose families have brought them to Mother because they are too poor to feed them.

Mother is very busy, but whenever she can, she spends time with the children. She plays with them, sings and dances with them, serves them their food and gives them all a hug and a kiss. The children feel that Mother is their own mother.

In addition to the orphanage, Mother has established numerous schools and institutions of higher education and computer training. She has established scholarship programs so that those who don't have much money can still get a higher education. Mother wants as many people as possible to get a good education, so they can get better jobs and help take care of their families.

Mother has also built hospitals for the poor; she has built thousands of houses for the homeless; she feeds the hungry; and she is helping people in countless other ways.

Mother says that the world is like a flower, and that all the different countries are the petals of that flower. Every year Mother travels to many countries all over the world, to the different petals of the world flower, to meet the tens of thousands of people who look upon her as their spiritual Master and Beloved Mother. She reaches out to those who are suffering and tries to help them. In her presence, people become kind-hearted, and those who are lonely discover that they have a Divine Friend who will always be there for them. Mother gives hope to those who are in despair, and she puts smiles on people's faces.

Mother teaches us that the most important thing in life is that we should love one another and take care of those who are less fortunate than ourselves. She inspires people to open their hearts to God. If we follow her advice, each of us can make this world a much happier, more loving place to live in.

Mother says: "A continuous stream of love flows from Mother towards all beings in the universe. That is Mother's inborn nature."

Part two

Experiences of Mother's children

Krishna's Crown

Takkali was a seven-year-old girl. She was Swami Purnamri-tananda's niece. Her real name was Sheeja, but Mother's pet name for her was "Takkali," which means tomato. Takkali had one wish which she had never told anyone. "O God," she prayed, "if you'd let me wear the crown that Mother wears during Krishna Bhava, I would be so happy!" But no one except Mother had ever worn that crown, and Takkali knew that her wish was impossible to fulfil.

On Krishna's birthday, Takkali went to the ashram with her parents. When she came on the little ferry boat across the back-waters to the ashram, she saw that Mother was standing at the boat jetty waiting for her. As soon as Takkali and her family got off the boat, Mother took Takkali by the hand and walked with her to the ashram. There they came upon a group of children dressed in colourful costumes. To celebrate Krishna's birthday, the children were going to perform a folk dance, which was a play about Krishna's childhood in Vrindavan. Mother lead Takkali into the temple and dressed her in beautiful clothes, the type of clothes that Krishna wore. Suddenly, to the little girl's delight, Mother placed the Krishna Bhava crown on Takkali's head! Now she looked just like Krishna when he was a child! Mother led Takkali outside, and made all the children stand in a ring, with Takkali standing in the middle. Then Mother asked them to dance around Takkali, as if she were Krishna. That was the happiest day of Takkali's life! She had never told Mother about her wish – but Mother knew everything, and she made Takkali's dream come true. God fulfils the wishes of those who are innocent and pure-hearted.

Dattan the Leper

Dattan was a leper. He was still a youth when he was stricken by the terrible disease, leprosy. When his parents discovered that their son was a leper, they threw him out of the house. His whole family turned against him and would have nothing to do with him. Because of his illness, Dattan couldn't get a job. So he became a beggar. He begged for his food and spent his days and nights on the grounds of a temple.

As time went by, his whole body became covered with sores of stinking pus. He lost all the hair on his head, and his eyes became so infected and swollen that there were only two slits where his eyes had been, and he was almost blind. People were disgusted when they saw him. They didn't want to have anything to do with him and even refused to give him any food. So he often had to go hungry.

He tried to cover his body with a big cloth, but this was very painful because the cloth would stick to his sores. Because of his

wounds, flies and other insects were constantly bothering him. He was never allowed to get on a bus, because people were so horrified by his illness. Not even the other beggars allowed him to go near them. At the mere sight of him, people held their noses and rushed away. Some even spat on him. Nobody cared about him. Never did Dattan hear a kind word from anyone. No one ever smiled at him or showed him any compassion. His life was a nightmare. He felt that he was the most worthless creature in the whole world.

Then, one day, he heard someone talking about the Holy Mother. Clinging to a tiny straw of hope, he decided to go and see her. He arrived one evening, during Devi Bhava, but no one would let him enter the temple to see Mother. He looked so ugly, with his face and body covered with sores, and he was stinking from all the pus. When the people saw him they told him to leave. "Go away!" they shouted at him. Dattan felt that his heart was breaking into a thousand pieces, for it seemed to him that even God hated him. But then suddenly, Mother caught sight of Dattan through the open doorway of the temple. She called out, "My son! My son! Come to me!"

Dattan went into the temple and shyly approached Mother, expecting her to show the same disgust as everyone else. But Mother didn't seem to notice how ugly he was, or the stench that came from his body. For the first time in more years than he could remember he was seeing a kind face – and Oh! – how much love and compassion there was on that face! Mother caressed him with great affection. She put her arms around him and held him close to her, as if he were the most adorable child on earth.

The people were shocked when they saw what Mother did next. Mother began to lick his pus-infected wounds, sucking the pus and blood from them, and spitting it out in a basin. She took the leper out to the backyard behind the temple and gave him a bath by pouring pots of water over his head. Then she put sacred ash all over his body, covering his sores with the ash. Dattan was overwhelmed by her motherly love. After that night, he came to see her during every Bhava *darshan*. Mother always went through the same ritual with him, licking his wounds, giving him a bath, and putting ash on his body. And each time she treated him with as much love as if he were her most beloved child. When Mother was asked by her devotees how she could do this, she replied, "Who else is there to take care of him and to love him? Amma doesn't see his external body; she sees only his heart. Amma cannot discard him. He is my son and I am his Mother. Can a mother abandon her child?"

Dattan became a changed man. Almost all his sores were healed. Mother's saliva was his divine medicine. His eyes were opened and he could see clearly again. The hair grew back on his head. Once again, he could travel freely on a bus without anyone being bothered by his presence. People talked to him and gave him food. Though the scars of the terrible disease still remained on Dattan's body, all the pus was gone and he no longer smelled bad. He could once again wear a shirt and a dhoti (loincloth) without the cloth sticking to his body, causing him pain. Thanks to Mother's grace, Dattan was happy. Mother gave him a new life.

Mother Heals a Paralysed Youth

In 1998, when Mother was visiting the United States, she heard about a youth who was staying in a hospital near Boston. He was completely paralysed. The youth, who was originally from India but whose family was now living in the US, had been walking down a street in Boston one day, when a large piece of scaffolding fell from a building that was under construction and landed on him. He was severely injured and had been paralysed ever since. There was nothing the doctors could do. His parents came to Mother while she was giving *darshan* in New York, and asked if it would be possible for her to go and see their son. Mother agreed. On her way from New York to Boston, Mother stopped at the hospital to see the boy. When Mother came into the room, he was sitting in a wheelchair. A chair had been specially arranged for Mother; the family had covered it with beautiful Indian silks. But Mother didn't seem to notice the chair. She went straight up to the boy and sat down on the floor in front of him. She gazed at him with an expression of infinite tenderness and caressed his useless legs. Then she took one of his feet into her hands and kissed it. She carefully put his foot down, then gently lifted his other foot and kissed it. The boy and his parents were so overwhelmed by Mother's love and humility that they wept. Even the swamis (monks and nuns) who were accompanying Mother were in tears. Mother stayed with the youth for a little while and then left for

Boston. Two hours later he discovered that he was able to walk! Thanks to Mother's grace he was completely cured.

Krishnan Unni's Operation

Krishnan Unni Nair lived in Los Angeles. His parents were deeply devoted to Mother. Whenever Mother came to Los Angeles, she would stay at their house.

When Krishnan Unni was five years old, he had to undergo a hernia operation. His parents were so worried about this that they sent a message to Mother in India. The day before the operation, Mother telephoned them and said, "My children, don't worry. There's absolutely nothing to worry about. Amma will be with Krishnan Unni during the operation."

The following day, Krishnan Unni was driven to the hospital. On the way, his parents told him stories about Mother and Krishna to make him feel better.

Just before he was wheeled into the operating theatre, Krishnan Unni's mother explained to him that she couldn't go in with him. She said, "Remember what Amma said on the phone yesterday – that you will be fine and that she will be with you."

"Yes," Krishnan Unni whispered.

A few hours later when he came out of the anaesthesia and woke up, his mother was sitting next to him. She smiled at him and said, "See, you are okay! Amma said that everything would be okay, didn't she?"

The little boy looked up at her and said, "I know, mom. I saw Amma. She was standing next to me the whole time with her hand on my shoulder."

Since then, Krishnan Unni and his family have moved to India. Krishnan Unni lives at the ashram in Amritapuri with his family. His father has become the medical executive of AIMS, Mother's state-of-the-art hospital.

A Little Girl Comes Back to Life

A little girl called Shayma lived near Mother. She suffered from severe asthma. One day Shayma had such a bad asthma attack that her grandmother rushed her to the hospital. But she reached there too late. Shayma was dead on arrival. When the doctors told the grandmother that her granddaughter was dead, the old woman was overcome with grief. She picked up the little body and carried it out of the hospital. She got on a bus and sat holding the dead girl in her lap all the way home.

When she reached the village, the old woman went straight to Mother's temple. Weeping loudly, she lay the dead child on the sacred seat on which Mother always sat during Devi Bhava. At that moment, Mother happened to be visiting another house where she was singing devotional songs. Mother suddenly felt very restless. She abruptly stopped singing and rushed over to the temple. There she found the old grandmother weeping and wailing beside the lifeless body of the child lying across the seat.

The old woman begged Mother to save the child. Mother sat down on the floor and lifted the body onto her lap. With the dead child lying in her lap, she began to meditate. Mother sat for a long time in meditation. Suddenly the little girl opened her eyes and gradually came back to life. Tears of joy streamed down the grandmother's face. Overwhelmed with gratitude, she embraced Mother again and again.

The Faith of a Child

In 1991 Mother visited Vancouver in Canada for three days. There the Herke family met Mother for the second time. One week later the Herkes were preparing to drive down to California, where Mother's programs were continuing. On the day they were going to leave, the parents of one of six-year-old Sharada Herke's school friends came to the school asking all the children to pray for their two-year-old son. Five days earlier he had fallen into a swimming pool. He had been under the water for at least five minutes. Though he was still alive, he had been in a coma for the entire five days. The doctors said that even if he recovered, he would certainly be brain damaged. But because five days had already gone by and he hadn't woken up, they didn't think he would survive at all. As Sharada and her family left for California, Sharada said, "I know what to do! I'll tell Mother about it."

When they arrived at the ashram, Mother was in Devi Bhava. Sharada went straight to Mother and told her about the little boy. Mother looked at Sharada for a long time and then said she would pray for him.

The next day Mother told Sharada that she felt the boy would be all right, and that Sharada was not to worry.

It wasn't until the family returned to Canada a few weeks later that they found out the rest of the story. On the same evening that Mother was told about the boy's accident, he suddenly woke up, perfectly healthy, as if he had just had a good night's sleep, although by this time he had been in a coma for six days. The doctors said it was a miracle. There was no evidence of any brain damage whatsoever, and the long rehabilitation program, which is normally required in such cases, was not needed at all in his case. All this happened because of Sharada's innocent faith. She felt that all she had to do was tell Mother about the little boy's accident and everything would be alright. And that is exactly what happened.

The Mango Tree

Not only human beings are Mother's children. Mother loves animals and plants just as much as she loves people. She is the Mother of all creatures. The following is the experience of one of Mother's children, who happens to be a tree.

One day some *brahmacharis* uprooted a young mango tree and planted it somewhere else. Unfortunately, the tree was in a state of shock from being moved, and the *brahmacharis* neglected it. So the tree wilted away and died. Some time later, Mother was out walking and happened to come across the dead tree. When she saw it her face was filled with pain. She bent down and kissed the tree. She was just like a mother with a hurt child. The *brahmacharis* noticed that her eyes were filled with tears. They were deeply moved when they saw her obvious love and compassion for nature, her deep concern for a little tree. And when they saw Mother's tears, they, too, started crying.

Mother said to them, "Children, please do not destroy life like this ever again. A person on the spiritual path should never do such a thing. Our goal is to experience life everywhere – to feel how everything is alive. We should try not to destroy something like this, because we have no right to destroy. Only God, who creates and takes care of everything, has the right to destroy. You must remember that everything is filled with consciousness and life. There is no such thing as mere matter – everything is conscious. God is everywhere."

When Mother had finished speaking, she hugged the tree and asked it to forgive the *brahmacharis* for what they had done. A few days later, the *brahmacharis* discovered that the tree had come back to life and was beginning to sprout new leaves. Mother's divine kiss and her love had awakened the dead tree.

A Flower For Krishna

Bhaskaran was one of Mother's neighbours. He was an elderly man who made a living by travelling from village to village, chanting the Srimad Bhagavatam and other scriptures, accepting whatever money was offered for his services. He had heard about Mother's Krishna Bhava and came a few times, but he was not really convinced that he was actually seeing Krishna himself during Krishna Bhava.

One night he had a vivid dream. Krishna appeared to him and said, "Son, you have been roaming around from village to village, holding me (the Srimad Bhagavatam) under your arm for so many years, and what have you gained? Here I am right under your nose in the house next door, and you do not recognize me. How foolish you are!" Bhaskaran woke up, startled. From then on he often went to Krishna Bhava.

One day, on his way back from a nearby village, he passed a pond next to a temple and was admiring the beauty of the lotus flowers floating on the water. He thought, "How nice it would be if I could offer one of those lotuses to Krishna during Krishna Bhava." He went to the priest of the temple and asked if he could pick a lotus flower as an offering to Krishna. Having received permission, he picked a beautiful pink lotus and started on his way to Mother's place.

Along the way, a charming little boy stopped him and begged him to give him the flower. Bhaskaran was in a dilemma. He felt an inexplicable attraction to the boy and felt a strong desire to give him the flower, to make him happy. But at the same time, he felt it would be wrong to give an ordinary person something that was intended for the worship of God. Finally, however, his heart won over his sense of duty, and he gave the little boy the lotus.

When he reached the ashram, Mother was already in Krishna Bhava. As soon as he entered the temple, she called him over to her side and smilingly asked, "Where is the flower?" Bhaskaran's heart jumped. He was so surprised that he couldn't say a word. Mother patted him affectionately on the head and said, "Don't worry, the little boy you gave the flower to – that was me, Krishna."

Jason

The first time Mother visited New York, she had just begun giving *darshan* one morning, when she pointed at a little blond boy, who was sitting with his father at the other side of the room. Mother said to one of the *brahmacharis*, "That child has no mother. Amma feels great love and compassion for him." The boy had not been up to Mother yet, and no one had told her anything about him.

After a while, Mother playfully tossed a chocolate across the room to where the little boy was sitting. He smiled and ate the chocolate. Soon after, Mother threw another chocolate halfway across the room. He walked a little closer to Mother and got his second treat. Mother repeated this a few more times and when he was close enough, Mother reached out and grabbed him. They both laughed. The little boy immediately felt a strong bond with Mother.

His father came up to Mother and explained that his son, Jason Richmond, who was six years old, had lost his mother when he was only eight months old; that he often woke up crying at night, asking why he didn't have a mother. Mother held Jason in her arms and said to him, "Jason, I am your Mother!" Jason gazed at Mother in wonder. He thought Mother meant that she was his mother who had given birth to him. His face shone with joy. For the first time in his life he was experiencing the love of a real mother – his very own. During the next few days, and during her subsequent visits to America each year, Mother showered Jason with love, making him feel that she was, indeed, his real mother.

On that first morning, Jason's father also told Mother that Jason suffered from epilepsy, that he had frequent seizures and that the medicine didn't help at all. Mother gave him a piece of sandalwood and instructed him on how to use it[8]. Mother's instructions were followed to the letter, and from then on, Jason never had another seizure.

---

[8] In India people make sandalwood paste. Mother often recommends it for different ailments.

Part three

Mother's teachings

1. My children, society needs people like you, who are young and intelligent. You represent the hope and the future of the world. Let the flower within you blossom, spreading its fragrance all over the world. Set out to wipe the tears of the suffering, and to spread the light of spirituality.

2. It is Mother's wish that all of Her children should dedicate their lives to spreading love and peace throughout the world. Real love and devotion for God is to have compassion for the poor and the suffering. My children, feed those who are hungry, help the poor, console the sorrowful, comfort the suffering, be charitable to all – this is Mother message to you.

3. Gold is so beautiful and precious. Imagine if gold also had a perfume – how much greater its value and charm would be! Meditation and other spiritual practices are very valuable indeed. But if, along with meditation and worship, we also try to develop such qualities as love, compassion and concern for our

fellow beings, it is like gold with a fragrance, something incredibly special and unique.

4. Once a master had a disciple who didn't like giving alms to the poor. The master knew this, and one day he went to the disciple's house disguised as a beggar. When he arrived, the disciple was busy worshipping the master's photo, offering milk and fruit before the picture. The master cried at the doorstep, "For the love of God, please give me some alms." The disciple drove him away, shouting, "There's nothing here for you!" The master immediately removed his disguise. When the disciple recognized his master, he was filled with remorse and asked his forgiveness.

Many people are just like the disciple in the story. They offer milk and fruit to a picture of God, but they refuse to offer even a handful of rice to a hungry man, not realizing that God dwells within that poor man. They are ready to love a picture of God, but not the living God.

5. Children, even if we are not in a position to help others materially, we can at least give them a loving smile or a kind word. It doesn't cost us anything. What is needed is a compassionate heart. This is the first step in spiritual life. Those who are kind and loving towards others have no need to wander in search of God, because God will come rushing to the heart that beats with compassion. Such a heart is God's favourite place to live.

6. *(Mother noticed that a brahmachari had not removed a banana peel that had been lying on the floor for a long time.)*
My son, you didn't pick up that banana peel even though you saw it lying there. If it is allowed to lie there, someone may accidentally slip on it and fall. It will then be your fault, won't it? – because you saw it and didn't remove it.

In the same way, you should also be alert while walking along a road. If there are any pieces of glass lying on the ground, they should be removed so that others won't hurt themselves. Those who are selfish won't care about such things. But we should take care so that even those who are selfish don't get hurt.

7. Why do we say "Om Namah Shivaya" when we greet people? "Om Namah Shivaya" means "Salutations to Shiva (the Auspicious One)." Every human being in this world is a part of God. So when we say "Om Namah Shivaya" to someone, we are saying to that person, "I greet the Divinity within you, and I want you to know that I love and respect that Divinity."

8. There was a girl who belonged to a wealthy family. She befriended a girl of her own age who came from a very poor family, and who also happened to be blind and lame. The rich girl loved that little girl; she was her best friend. She played with her every day, and was always trying to cheer her up and make her laugh. But the rich girl's father wasn't pleased at all when he discovered that his daughter was playing with a girl from a poor family. He wanted her to forget that girl and instead make friends with other children of the same background as herself. So he invited the daughter of one of his wealthy friends to come and play with his daughter. Even though the two girls became good friends, the girl was still much more fond of her little blind friend, and much preferred her company. When her father found out about this, he asked her, "Why do you want to be friends with a girl who is so poor, when you already have my wealthy friend's daughter as your friend?" She replied, "Oh, father, I do like that other girl very much. But she has plenty of toys and other friends to play with. My friend here is all alone. If I don't love her and show her a little kindness, she will have no one else who cares about her. I want to help her."

Children, we should always remember that all people are the same, the top people in society as well as the people at the bottom. But the very existence of those who are extremely poor depends on the love and compassion of others. A wealthy person usually has a lot of support from others, but a very poor person is looked down upon by almost everyone, except a few goodhearted people.

9. All things such as money and worldly objects are gone forever when you give them away – but not love. Because the more love you give, the more your heart will be filled with love. Love is like a never-ending stream. Mother wants all of her children to become sources of love, always spreading love and compassion amongst their fellow beings, and thereby teaching others to do the same.

10. Someone asked Mother, "Why does God keep quiet when people are suffering so much? Can't he do something to take the suffering away?"

But God *has* done something about it. He has created us, hoping that we will do something to help those who are suffering. We should think of those people. We should try to feel their suffering. We should try to put ourselves in their place. We tend to think only of our own problems. We do not care about the problems of others, nor do we feel any compassion. That is our biggest problem.

11. There was once a king whose country was constantly being attacked by neighbouring countries, and he was always losing against them. As they attacked his borders, he was losing his kingdom, bit by bit. One day he felt that he couldn't take it anymore. He decided to give up. He gave up his duties as a king and retired to a forest. He was feeling very depressed. One day he saw a small spider trying to weave a web between two branches of a tree. Again and again the spider tried to connect its threads between the branches, but without any success, because the spider web kept breaking. But even though the spider kept failing, it refused to give up. The king watched with growing fascination

as the little insect continued to work diligently. It even jumped over to the other branch and tried to connect the web from the other side. Finally, after many attempts, the spider succeeded in spinning and weaving a strong, beautiful web between the two branches.

The king learned a great lesson from that little spider. He thought, "If even a seemingly insignificant spider can try so hard without ever giving up, then surely I should be able to do the same, and work harder at my royal duties, without giving up when things get tough, and running away like a coward." And thus, the king returned to his kingdom and assumed his role as king. From then on he refused to give up. Through sheer determination, he bravely defeated each one of the neighbouring countries that tried to attack his kingdom, until they no longer dared to attack him. And finally his country enjoyed peace. He ruled his kingdom justly and wisely for many years, and he never forgot the lesson the little spider had once taught him.

12. No work is unimportant or meaningless. It is the amount of love – the amount of heart that you pour into your work – that makes it significant and beautiful.

13. Gaining mastery over your mind is the most important education you can get. That is spiritual education.

14. Even the "selfishness" of a spiritual person will benefit the world. There were two boys living in a village. Both of them were given some seeds by a visiting monk. The first boy roasted his seeds and ate them, thus appeasing his hunger. He was a worldly person. The second boy sowed his seeds in the ground and thereby produced a lot of grain, which he gave to people who were hungry. Even though both boys had the initial selfishness to accept what was given to them, the second boy's attitude benefited many people.

15. Your heart is a shrine – and that is where God should be installed. Good thoughts are the flowers that you offer to God; good deeds are your worship of him; whenever you speak kindly to others, you are singing a hymn to God; and your love is the sacred food that you offer him.

16. Children, you should never do anything that could cause anyone pain or suffering. Such actions will have a bad effect on you. Often, when we hurt someone, that person is innocent. With aching hearts, such people will exclaim that you have hurt them even though they have done nothing wrong. Their thoughts and prayers will affect you, and will later become the cause of suffering for you. That is why it is emphasized that one should never hurt others by thought, word or deed. Even if we cannot give joy to others, we should at least refrain from causing them any pain. If we are careful in this matter, God's grace will be with us.

17. Once a government minister visited a village, which happened to be the dirtiest village in the whole country. He spent a night as the guest of the mayor of the village. Piles of garbage lay heaped everywhere along the roads, and the open drains were filled with filthy, stagnant waste water. The whole village was permeated with a terrible stench.

The minister asked the mayor why the place was so dirty. The mayor said, "The people of this village are ignorant. They don't know anything about cleanliness. They simply don't care. I've tried to teach them, but they won't listen. I've told them to clean the village, but they won't do it. So I've given up." The mayor went on and on, blaming the villagers. The minister listened patiently without saying anything. They had dinner and then the minister went to bed.

Early the next morning, when the mayor woke up, he went to invite the minister for breakfast, but discovered that his guest was gone. The mayor looked everywhere and asked his servants if they had seen the minister, but no one knew where he was. Everyone started looking for him. At last the mayor found him. The minister was out on the road, cleaning up the rubbish all by himself. He was heaping the rubbish into a big pile and setting it on fire. When he saw this, the mayor felt ashamed. He said to himself, "How can I stand here doing nothing, when the minister himself is working like this?" So he joined him and started cleaning up the village. When the villagers came out into the streets, they were surprised to see the two men doing such dirty work. They felt that they couldn't just stand there and watch while the minister and the mayor were cleaning up the village. So they joined in the work. In no time, the whole village was spotlessly clean. All the rubbish had been removed and the drains were clean. There was not a speck of rubbish to be seen. The whole village looked completely different.

Children, to teach something by one's own example takes much less time than trying to teach by preaching about it. Do not stand around pointing your finger at others, criticizing them for not doing what needs to be done. Take the initiative and set an example by doing it yourself. Then others will naturally follow your example. Blaming others will not change anyone. If you criticize others, your own mind will become polluted, and no good will come of it. Action is what is needed. Only if you, yourself, try to do something, will there be a change for the better.

18. We should always forgive others their faults. If people criticize us and blame us for something we haven't done, we usually react and get angry. We should simply forgive them. God is testing us, and he is also testing those who offend us. Never get angry with anyone.

19. Those who harm others out of selfishness are in fact digging a pit into which they themselves will fall. It is like spitting in the air while lying on your back: the spit will fall on your own face.

20. Children, failures are bound to happen in life. Suppose you were to stumble over something and fall. You wouldn't say to yourself, "All right! Now that I've fallen, I'll just continue to lie here on the ground forever. I'm not going to get up and continue." It would be silly to think like that, wouldn't it?

A little toddler will fall countless times before he or she has learned to walk properly. In the same way, failures are a natural part of life. Keep in mind that each failure comes with the message of potential success. Just as a toddler will fall before he or she learns to walk with firm steps, our own failures are the beginning of our ascent towards ultimate victory. So there is no need to feel disappointed or frustrated.

21. Once there was a man who boarded a train carrying a large, heavy suitcase on his head. After the train had started on its way, the man, struggling with the weight of the suitcase, began to cry, "Oh my! The weight of this luggage is too much to bear!"

Hearing this, a nearby passenger asked, "Then why don't you just put the luggage down? Let the train carry the weight for you."

Similarly, when we surrender everything at God's feet, we no longer need to worry about our lives. God will carry all of our burdens for us.

22. If we look at the lives of Rama, Krishna, Buddha and Jesus Christ, we can see that they faced many obstacles in their lives. But because they acted with patience and enthusiasm, they were able to succeed.

Of course, some people may argue and say that they were great mahatmas, and that we cannot compare ourselves with them — that we are just ordinary people, so how could we possibly try to be like them? But Mother says that we are not just ordinary beings. We are extraordinary. There is an infinite power within each of us. We are not just little batteries – we have a direct connection to the Power Source itself. We must learn to bring out this power, to cultivate it and realize it. Then, we, too, will be successful in life.

23. Children, if each one of us makes the effort, we can get rid of the poverty in our country.

24. If there are at least two youths in a village or a neighbourhood who will try to serve the world, taking the initiative to organize service activities and to spread spiritual wisdom, the world will change for the better.

25. We can learn so much from the example of nature by watching and seeing how easily nature overcomes any obstacles. For instance, if there is a stone in the path of a tiny ant, the ant just walks over or around the stone and continues on its way. Or if there is a rock in the way where a tree is growing, the tree will simply grow around the rock. In the same way, the water of a river flows around a log or a big rock that is blocking its path. We, too, should learn to adapt to all the circumstances in life, learning to overcome them, with patience and enthusiasm.

26. If someone happens to scold us or quarrel with us, we get angry with that person. We may even physically attack him or her because of our enmity. But the sages feel no enmity towards anyone. They even love those who are against them. That is what the sages and other noble characters of the Indian epics were like.

27. If a seed is to grow and become a big tree, it first has to go down beneath the earth. Only through modesty and humility can we grow spiritually. Pride and selfishness will only destroy us. Be loving and compassionate, with the attitude that you are the servant of everyone. The whole universe will then bow down to you.

28. In a cyclone, large trees are uprooted and buildings collapse. But no matter how strong the cyclone is, it cannot damage a lowly blade of grass. This is the greatness of humility.

29. Children, if you are leaving the house on some errand, pay your respects to your elders before you go. Make it a habit to take leave of your parents before going to school in the morning. God pours his grace on those who are humble.

30. What this world needs are servants, not leaders. Everyone wishes to become a leader. We have enough leaders who are not real leaders. Let us become real servants instead. For that is the only way to become a real leader.

31. God is in everything, not just in human beings. God is in the mountains, the rivers and the trees, in the birds and the animals, in the clouds, the sun, the moon and the stars.

Everything in nature has a purpose to fulfil. There are no mistakes in God's Creation. Every creature and every object that has been created by God is so utterly special. How can anyone who understands this want to kill and destroy?

32. Children, think of the wonderful miracles of nature! Camels are blessed with a special bag in which they can store water during their long treks through the desert. The kangaroo has a built-in cradle, so that it can carry its baby wherever it goes. Even the most seemingly unimportant creature, even harmful ones, have a special part to play in the world. For example: spiders keep the insect population in balance, snakes keep the rats from becoming too many, and even the tiny plankton in the sea serve as food for the whales. Many plants look like useless weeds, but they can be made into medicines that can cure terrible diseases. We do not know the purpose of everything. Mother Nature is a mystery to us. Without nature, no creature, no human beings

or anything else could live. So it is our duty to lovingly care for all living things.

33. Plants and trees have feelings too. They can even feel afraid. When someone goes up to a tree with an axe, the tree feels so afraid that it trembles. You cannot see it, but if you have a compassionate heart, you will feel it.

34. Experience is the teacher of each person. Suffering, my children, is the teacher that brings you closer to God.

35. Look for the good in everyone. Be like the honeybee that gathers only honey wherever it goes.

36. We become mentally weak when we look at the faults of others, but we rise to a higher level when we choose to see the goodness in everyone. Whoever it may be, when we say that a person is bad, we have already become bad ourselves. Ninety-nine percent of a person may be at fault, yet we should see the one single percent of goodness in him or her. Then we ourselves will become good. If we look at the negative side of a person, we are lowering ourselves. We should always pray, "O God, make my eyes see only the good in everyone. Give me the strength to serve the world selflessly." Only through such an attitude of self-surrender can we experience any real peace of mind. Thus slowly we should try to become God's good servants.

37. Suppose we fall into a hole. Do we get angry at our eyes and poke them because they didn't guide us properly? No, of course not. And just as we patiently endure the mistakes made by our own eyes, we should bear with others if they fail and make mistakes, and we should always be kind to them.

38. Even while someone is cutting down a tree, the tree provides him with shade. This is what a spiritual person should be

like. Only someone who prays for the welfare of others, even of those who make him suffer, can truly be called a spiritual person.

39. If a person does a hundred good things and makes just one mistake, people will despise him and reject him. But if a person makes a hundred mistakes and does just one good thing, God will love him and accept him. That is why you should be attached to God alone. Dedicate everything to him.

40. There is only one God. Milk is known by different names in different languages. A man from Kerala calls it "paal." An Englishman calls it "milk." People who speak other languages have other names for milk. Whatever the name, the colour and taste is the same. Christians call God Christ; Muslims call Him Allah; Hindus may call him Shiva, Krishna or the Divine Mother. It is the same God. Each person understands God according to his own culture and worships him accordingly.

41. Even small children can benefit by practicing meditation. Their intellect will become brilliant and they'll develop tremendous memory power. This will help them greatly in their studies.

42. Meditating and doing spiritual practices doesn't just mean sitting in a lotus posture with your eyes closed. It also means to selflessly serve people who are suffering, to console those who are in distress, to smile at someone and to say a few loving words.

43. People often do not care if others are having a difficult time. Their attitude is, "Let someone else suffer, as long as it's not me." Let us change this attitude. Let us instead sincerely wish that no one in the world should have to suffer. Let us not think, "Why me?" but rather, "Why should anyone have to suffer?" Let us learn to put others before ourselves.

44. Humility is the sign of true knowledge.

45. All of us are different forms of the one Self, like the same types of toffee wrapped in different coloured papers. The toffee covered with a green wrapper may tell the toffee with a red wrapper, "I am different from you." And the toffee in red paper may tell the toffee in a blue paper, "You and I are different." But once the wrappers are removed, all the toffees are exactly the same. In the same way, there is no real difference between people. Whether we are rich or poor, brown or white, beautiful or ugly, healthy or sick – inside we are all the same. But we forget this and are deluded by what we see on the outside. It is because of this delusion that we are creating problems in today's world.

46. Mother has a strong wish that all of her children will become so pure that they will spread light and love to whomever they meet. It is not preachers, but living examples that this world needs now.

47. Children, always remember that your true family is the world family, the family of humankind. If you happen to injure your left hand, your right hand will come to its aid. This is because both hands are parts of your own body; you feel that you are one with them. It is with the same spirit of oneness that we should love and serve all our brothers and sisters in this world. We should forgive them their faults, and we should even be willing to suffer for their sake. That is the very essence of spirituality.

48. Children, instead of pointing at others and criticizing them, try to correct yourselves first.

49. There is love and Love. You love your family, but you do not love your neighbour. You love your father and mother, but you do not love everyone the way you love your father and mother. You love your religion, but you do not love all religions; you may even dislike people of other faiths. You love your country, but you do not love all countries. That is not true Love; it is only

limited love. The transformation of this limited love into Divine Love is the goal of spirituality. In the fullness of Love blossoms the beautiful, fragrant flower of compassion.

50. If you take one step towards God, you will experience that God takes a hundred steps toward you.

Om Amriteshwaryai Namaha